THE WINNING SPIRIT

THE
WINNING SPIRIT

Life Lessons Learned in Last Place

ZOE KOPLOWITZ
WITH MIKE CELIZIC

DOUBLEDAY
NEW YORK • LONDON • TORONTO • SYDNEY • AUCKLAND

PUBLISHED BY DOUBLEDAY
a division of Bantam Doubleday Dell Publishing Group, Inc.
1540 Broadway, New York, New York 10036

DOUBLEDAY and the portrayal of an anchor with a dolphin are trademarks of
Doubleday, a division of Bantam Doubleday Dell Publishing Group, Inc.

Library of Congress Cataloging-in-Publication Data

Koplowitz, Zoe.
    The winning spirit: life lessons learned in last place / Zoe
Koplowitz with Mike Celizic. — 1st ed.
        p.   cm.
    1. Koplowitz, Zoe.   2. Runners (Sports)—United States—Biography.
3. Physically handicapped athletes—United States—Biography.
4. New York City Marathon, New York, N.Y.   5. Running for the
handicapped.   6. Multiple sclerosis—Patients—United States—
Biography.   I. Celizic, Mike.   II. Title.
GV1061.15.K67A3   1997
362.1′96834′0092—dc21
[B]   97-21799
                                                               CIP

ISBN 0-385-48987-0
November 1997

10   9   8   7   6   5   4   3   2   1

First Edition

For Hester
Year after year, we have turned every challenge into a victory
and together we've reinvented the word "magic."
Thank you for teaching me so much about "The Winning Spirit."
Thank you for being my best friend

For Mike Celizic and Tom Connor
Who knew a good story when they heard one
And never backed down and never gave up till it had been told.
Thank you for believing

For Tiger Information Systems . . .
You are all my "Good Job Karma" finally come full cycle.
Thank you for all your support and unconditional love

For all of you who have joined us on the road,
Either in body or in spirit
Thank you for playing such an important part in the adventure.
This book is dedicated to you . . .
With Gratitude and Blessings.
Love,
ZOE

To the memory of George W. Baker,
who loved a good adventure.
—M.C.

ACKNOWLEDGMENTS

OF ALL THE gifts that life can give us, perhaps friendship is the most profound. For all your laughter, love, and wisdom, and just for being you, I'd like to acknowledge the following:

Frances Jones, editor extraordinaire, and all the fine folks at Doubleday; Dick Traum and Les Winter, and all my brothers and sisters at the Achilles Track Club; Jill Luteyn, Vice President, Chase Manhattan Bank; Judy Adler and Diane Filippi, DEF Public Relations; Arnay Rosenblat, good friend and tireless advocate, National MS Society; Curtis Sliwa, Pete Cozo, and the NYC Guardian Angels; Grete Waitz, Bill Rogers, and the NYC Road Runners Club; Ben and Edith Herman, Marsha Kessler, Michael Warren, and Karen Robinson, fellow pilgrims along the road; Rich Mauch and the Marathon Strides Team, NYC MS Society; Charles Koplowitz; The Peppas Clan, Wendy and Steve, Christian and Evelyn; Carol Ellis; Justin Gennaro; Ruth Messinger; Mark McQueen; Steve Leeds, Rachel Hott, and my Tuesday NLP classmates.

Would but there were time and space, there would be at least another hundred names on this list. So for all of you whose names do not appear in print, know that you are loved and valued.

—Zoe

THIS IS THE part that always feels like the Academy Awards—so many people to thank, so little time. It starts with Zoe, a terrific writer, a pleasure to work with, and a good friend. You wrote a hell of a book, Zoe. I'm grateful to have had the opportunity to be a part of it.

There's Rita Enders, who took on a big transcription job on short notice and turned in remarkable work. Without her, this book would not exist. I want also to thank Dr. Dennis Scharfenberg and Dr. John Scheuch, without whose care and skill I would not exist. My editor at *The Record,* Gabe Buonauro, and his multitalented assistant, John Rowe, put up with me, which is no small achievement. Thanks to Tom Connor, the agent who never gave up.

There is no way I can ever so much as begin to express the enormous debt of gratitude and love I owe my wife, Margaret A. Sinnott, as fine a woman as there is. Whatever part of this book I am responsible for is as much her work as it is mine. And to Carl, Jim, Jane, and the Zack-Man, thanks for being your wonderful selves.

—M.C.

THE WINNING SPIRIT

CHAPTER 1

IT IS LATE July. Sweltering. Humid. Obnoxious. Clothes stick to your body like Saran Wrap. Tempers are short and bad attitude is everywhere. Like the humidity, it creeps, it seeps, and it invades. By the end of the day, it permeates even the kindest of hearts and the gentlest of spirits. Summertime—and the livin' ain't easy. Welcome to urban America.

There is a water main break that disables two of the major subway systems. At any time of day this would be considered a grave inconvenience. Right before rush hour it is tantamount to catastrophe. Needless to say, it is right before rush hour. Welcome to New York City.

I find heat and humidity totally intolerable. It is a devastating combination that reduces me to my worst common denominator—weak and exhausted. And now, with the subway out of service, the buses will be jam-packed with angry, sweaty rush-hour commuters. I can count on the trip home taking at least an additional hour. And to top it all off, there will be standing room only. Insult to injury. Welcome to my life.

As I board the Sixth Avenue bus headed uptown, I am a study in resignation. One more disastrous day in what is turning out to be a disastrous life. Par for the course. No more and no less. Total surrender to the unpredictable caprices of life on planet Earth. It's not a conscious choice. It appears to be the only remaining course of action.

The bus is a self-fulfilling prophecy. It is everything I feared it would be, and then some. Sardine City. Moist and smelly and vacuum-packed.

Idly, I contemplate my limited knowledge of college biochemistry. I ponder the melting point of the human body. It seems logical to me that those of us stuck on this bus have undoubtedly surpassed that point already. Perhaps I have inadvertently discovered a new Law of Thermodynamics: Zoe's Law. I fantasize about melting into the person next to me. We become one big, inextricable blob of gelatinous material. A Technicolor Jell-O vat.

My reverie ends abruptly, as a fellow passenger collapses against me. Instinctively, I reach out to catch him. So does the man next to me. The best we are able to do is break his fall. I get a fleeting glimpse of sparse gray hair and an ancient, careworn face, of brown slacks and a short-sleeved shirt. As he falls to the floor, we take infinite care that he does not hit his head. It is the very least we can do for this unfortunate stranger.

Right after he falls, all hell breaks loose on the bus. The air is punctuated with shouts and curses—a volatile mixture of fear and rage. How could he have the audacity to collapse in the middle of rush hour, further complicating everyone's journey home? It isn't as if we can throw him off the bus and keep on going! Now this bus will be out of service and stuck here forever, a virtual guarantee that the next bus will be even more crowded and obnoxious.

Probably nothing motivates large groups of people to action quite as quickly or as well as does fear. People start jumping over the man to get off the bus. There is an inordinate amount of pushing, shoving, and jostling. You'd think that they were fleeing the sinking *Titanic,* not merely exiting the Sixth Avenue bus.

It isn't that I'm braver or stronger than everyone else. Not by a long shot. Perhaps I'm even more terrified than those who flee. But fear and I have had more than a nodding acquaintance in my lifetime. And you might say that in these last few months, we've become downright intimate.

If I've learned nothing else at all in life, I've learned that you can't run away from that which you fear. Flee from one set of circumstances, and sooner or later a similar set is bound to track you down. Flight doesn't do it. Neither does wishful thinking. Ignore it, and it doesn't go away. It only looms larger and brighter, and sooner or later it will have its way with you. That which you resist persists.

I drop down on the floor next to him. I hold his hand and stroke his cheek. I am a still life in commiseration and concern. Initially, I assume he has succumbed to the heat. I can deal with this if I need to. Within a minute or two, the bus is empty. Only the bus driver, myself, and the recumbent, semiconscious stranger remain.

He moves his head from side to side. Almost imperceptibly. His face is ashen and his eyes are wild with pain and fear. With sinking stomach and pounding heart, I realize for the first time that this is not just a case of heat exhaustion.

And then, there is the sound—a gargling, gasping sound that resonates from the very center of his being. It is a sound as ancient as humanity itself. It is the final chord in the symphony of human life. Discordant and compelling. Even if you have never heard it before, you recognize it instantly. It is the sound of death.

He looks puzzled. His eyebrows arch, and his eyes momentarily narrow, searching for the source of that sound. Then, a final, long, slow exhalation that ends with the syllable *oh*. The puzzle is solved. The fear is gone. In its place there is knowledge and acceptance of the inevitable.

For a brief moment our eyes meet. A solitary tear trickles down the side of his face. I continue to hold on to him, stroking him, comforting him and reassuring him that I will not abandon him.

He moves his head one final time, and his expression is transformed. Worry and care are dissipated. Facial lines are erased, as if by magic. His gaze shifts to a distant point beyond my range of vision. And in that moment, I believe that he sees whatever is on the other side of his earthly existence. He has, as the euphemism goes, "met his Maker." The spirit has begun its final journey home, and the body can not help but follow in its wake.

There are no extraordinary measures I can take to save his life or to bring him back. CPR has not yet become a technique familiar to average people on a New York City bus; it won't for another ten years. Today, I would probably be all process and technology, a human Red Cross manual in action—complete with chest compressions and rescue breathing. At that moment, the best I can give is the most basic of human offerings. The gifts of touch and comfort.

I know that he is dead, and still I cannot leave him. Someone must be there, to value him and care for him in these moments before the police and ambulance arrive. I remain on the floor, holding his hand. With the meeting of our eyes, my word was given, and I will keep it. I will not abandon him.

His eyes remain open and sightless. I cannot close them,

for with that simple gesture I feel I would, in some way I cannot fully comprehend, make his death final. It is a task best left to the dispassionate hands of a stranger, the post facto ministration of one who has not touched his face or held his hand in his final moments.

The police arrive. As is mandated by the difficulties of their jobs, they are a study in emotional detachment and bureaucratic intervention. Ballpoint pens and pocket-size notebooks materialize. There are forms to be filled out. Questions to be asked. Answers to be given.

This, by their standards, is a gentler, kinder death than most of the street scenarios they have witnessed in the course of their careers. "Old guy," they observe. "Heart attack? Stroke? Who knows? Coroner will figure it out. You can probably rule out foul play. Poor old bastard probably never even knew what hit him."

They close his eyes and go through his pockets. A wallet is excavated. I wait for information. None is forthcoming. I am told that, since we're not related, the information is confidential, pending notification of next of kin. This is reasonable but unacceptable. I persist and they resist.

"What's it to you?" they ask. "I was here when he died," I explain, "and I need for him to have a name. Oh, God, I really need for him to have a name." A young cop, probably not much older than I am, bends down, ostensibly to offer me a hand in getting up from the floor. He whispers in my ear, "Joseph. His name is Joseph."

Most of us are delivered into the world at the hands of a total stranger. More often than not, we are eased off the planet in a similar manner. The former is exalted, and the latter is mourned. Such are the dictates of culture and tradition.

Before I allow myself to be helped up from the floor of the bus, I pat Joseph's hand and touch his face one final time. "Joseph," I whisper to him, "my name is Zoe."

Now we are strangers no longer. We are, at the very least, on a first-name basis. It is appropriate familiarity for traveling companions who have shared an intimate journey with such an unforeseen destination. He is Joseph and I am Zoe. He did not die alone and he did not die grasping the hand of a total stranger on the Sixth Avenue bus.

On leaving the bus, I'm so overcome with emotion that I can barely walk. There are a hundred unanswerable questions hurtling around in my brain at warp speed. Who are you, Joseph, and where were you going on this hot summer day? What appointment or rendezvous will remain forever unattended? In your lifetime, who knew you as a friend? Who embraced you as a lover?

Is there a "Mrs. Joseph" waiting at home who will miss your touch, your scent, your smile? Or has she gone before you and, by current consensus of belief, now waits for you at journey's end? What snapshot of your life will be forever mounted in the photo album of time and memory? I wish I could know. And I know I never will.

And what of my own life? What's to become of me? Where do I go from here, and how in God's name will I ever get there?

Standing on the sidewalk, I flash back to that ominous doctor's appointment of four months ago. I can still smell the hospital disinfectant. I can still see the doctor's face. It could have happened a half-hour ago. The outcome remains intractable.

.   .   .

THE NEUROLOGIST IS shuffling papers around in my folder, as though, by changing the order of the papers, he can magically alter their contents. His inhalations are staccato bursts, his exhalations long and slow. He is blowing imaginary smoke rings. I know this for a fact. I have seen my father do it on countless occasions when his nemesis, the NO SMOKING sign, prohibited indulgence. It is the respiration pattern of a two-pack-a-day smoker. The doctor would probably give just about anything to have a cigarette right now. To tell the truth, so would I. And I don't even smoke.

He has not so much as glanced in my direction since I entered the office. No reassuring words. No eye contact. No nothing. By my standards, this does not bode well. I still hope for the best, but his body language and evident discomfort imply the worst.

There is an interminable silence. The gears of my life come to a grinding halt. When he finally speaks, he says the words that will forever alter the course of my life.

"Do you want it straight?"

"No," I quip, "I'd prefer it on the rocks." He doesn't laugh. He doesn't even smile. And in that moment I know for sure. My fate is sealed. All is lost.

"I'm sorry to have to tell you," he says, "that you have multiple sclerosis. It is a degenerative neurological disease. We don't know what causes it, and, to be quiet truthful, we don't know how to cure it. There are steroids and other drugs that we can give you to try to control the symptoms, but, to be honest, they sometimes create as many problems as they solve. But we'll cross that bridge when we come to it.

"Will you get worse? Hard to know for sure. Some people do and others don't, and once again we just don't know why. Worst-case scenario? You could lose your eyesight, the ability to walk, your bladder or bowel control. Or you could remain pretty much the way you are right now. Could you die? Yes, I suppose you could. But there's no reason to put the cart before the horse.

"The best you can do for yourself is make adjustments in your life. No stress. No unnecessary physical activity. Keep a quiet lifestyle, a good attitude, and hope for the best. And if you're religious, pray. By all means, pray."

He spends an additional ten minutes schooling me in the parlance of the neurologically defunct. There is talk of nerves and myelin sheathes and prednisone and optic neuritis. Ad infinitum. It is an introductory course to the rest of my life.

The problem is that this can't possibly by *my* life. I know what *my* life looks like, and it certainly doesn't look like *this*. Perhaps I've been catapulted into some other dimension and have landed in the middle of someone else's life. Or maybe I'm asleep and this is the ultimate nightmare. I will wake up, and it will all go away. Long shot, but I'll take it. So, totally against the dictates of common sense, I pinch myself. Hard. Really hard. I do not wake up. It does not go away. So much for long shots.

The neurologist is still talking. It doesn't matter. I have heard as much as I'm willing or able to hear for one day. In my head, I construct a linear equation. No cause + no cure + no help + no hope = death. In the weeks to follow, that equation will transform itself into a never-ending mantra. It will haunt my sleep like some primitive, wordless funeral dirge, keening and wailing and weeping. It will punctuate my every waking hour with that most unanswerable of all questions. Why me, God? Why me?

It is 1973. I am twenty-five years old. I am not a happy camper.

The first three months after my diagnosis are probably the hardest months. I feel that I am no longer author or star of the most precious production of all—my own life. A new director has been hired. Its name is multiple sclerosis. Script changes have been made without my knowledge or consent. The plot has been sabotaged and the characters altered beyond recognition. The heroine remains stoic and valiant, but tragic and moribund. She is, at best, fatally flawed.

My internal dialogue becomes flagrant plagiarism of every three-hankie movie I have ever seen. I am Bette Davis in *Dark Victory*. I am Irene Dunne in *Magnificent Obsession*. I am Deborah Kerr in *An Affair to Remember*. I wither. I wane. I wilt. But, oddly enough, I do not die. Not even close.

Invariably, in those first few months, my Oscar-losing performance gives way to a stand-up comedy routine of sorts. My life becomes the ultimate good news–bad news joke. The punch line changes daily. The good news is that I'm still alive—more or less. Some days more, some days less. The bad news is that I remain obsessed with my rapidly deteriorating relationship with God.

At the time, I was a novitiate minister in a religious community known as the Foundation Faith of God. In 1973 much of the world was in "search mode." Even the Beatles. We were all in pursuit of that elusive person or philosophy that would give our lives meaning and spiritual value. The Beatles found their Swami What's-His-Face, and I found the Foundation.

On entering the Foundation, as was required, I had given up my apartment, my job, and all the accoutrements of middle-class life. I was permitted to maintain contact with my family and friends, but there was seldom the time or energy to do so.

I was also required to choose a new name for myself, to be selected on the basis of its meaning. It would serve as a daily verbal affirmation of the new reality and lifestyle I had chosen.

As a kid, I had always had a theory about the letter Z. I believed that of all the letters in the alphabet, God love Z the best, that is why He saved it for last. I thought that the capital Z was a beautiful, magical letter because you could write it so many ways. Plain or fancy. Loops or swirls. Or just like Zorro—big and bold and *in your face*. I was convinced that I would someday have my very own special Z name. A self-fulfilling prophecy that comes to pass for a totally different set of reasons. My childhood daydream had become an adult reality. I had chosen the name Zoe. It means life.

My intention when I joined the Foundation was to live in a community setting, and, within the context of that extended family framework, to make a difference in the world. At the time, I viewed the Foundation as a kind of religious Urban Peace Corps. I was an Aquarian prophetess preaching the New Age gospel of healing and wholeness to the indigent populations of North America.

During that period of time, the Foundation operated an upscale coffee house on the Upper East Side of New York

City. No shabby sublets or roach-infested rentals for them. They owned the building. Even by 1990s' standards, they would have been considered a very classy group of well-educated, multitalented individuals. They offered an endless array of workshops, lectures, and prominent guest speakers on healing, meditation, nutrition, and wellness in all its various aspects. They became a definitive resource center for lessons on the ins and outs of all things New Age-y.

You would have thought this seemingly progressive, enlightened community of fellow seekers would be a source of comfort and empowerment in the face of an MS diagnosis. Oddly enough, the direct opposite was true. I was subjected to an endless battery of questions, all of which strongly suggested that I had in some way violated the moral edicts of the community, and this was divine retribution at its hell-bent best.

WHEN DIVINE DISTRESS was finally ruled out as a direct cause of my illness, we entered into what I thought of as Phase Two, the convoluted Catch-22 doctrine of "personal responsibility." And it has more wrinkles than a Sharpei puppy.

Since God had nothing to do with my MS, it was reasoned, then I had obviously created it myself. If I had created it, I could choose to uncreate it. If I failed to uncreate it, then I was doing what was known as "performing." Performing was viewed as an unconscious attempt to divert vital energy from community goals and the common good and in order to gain individual attention. Any kind of illness, no matter how serious or legitimate, was considered performing.

The Foundation felt that the best way it could support

me was to make sure that I received no perks for having MS. I was given no rest periods, no special privileges of any kind; I was frequently required to work longer and harder than anyone else. My entire life became an excruciating exercise in apology and overcompensation.

Presumably, this was an act of love, done for my own good. It was to help me stop performing and, as the saying goes, "get off it." My unquestioning compliance was viewed as a daily testament to my devotion to God and my commitment to the community.

While no one ever directly told me that I was not allowed to talk about my MS, instinctively I understood that any discussion of it would be seen as performing. As cheerful and acquiescent as I remained, I could never again be part of their picture-perfect world. In a community that held healing as its central tenet, I had become a pariah in every sense of the word. Appearances were everything, and my spastic, cane-assisted gait left much to be desired.

I was informed that I would never be ordained into the next level of the hierarchy as long as I had MS. When I protested, I was reprimanded. Severely. How could I be so selfish? If my priorities were in alignment with the good of the community, I would accept this as a justifiable consequence of my obstinate need to remain incurably ill.

As far as I was concerned, the life of a perpetual novitiate was no life at all. It was an existence devoid of initiative and possibility; it relegated me for all time to the most menial of chores and the most subservient of demeanors.

In addition to the spiritual ramifications of my plight, there were straightforward, practical matters to be considered. I had no money, no apartment, no job, and no health insurance. In essence, I had become what I most feared: impoverished, homeless, unemployed, and seriously ill.

In my daily prayers, I was shameless. I begged. I cajoled. I blamed. I plea-bargained. Dear God, why have You done this to me? What have I ever done to You that could have pissed You off this badly? I'm twenty-five years old. My life is just beginning, and now it's all over. Please, please help me, I prayed. Send me a sign. Just a little one. No need to raise the dead. No need to walk on water. No miracles. Nothing fancy. Just a little something to let me know you're still on my side. Just give me another chance. I swear to You, I'll do better. Just one more chance . . .

No answer was forthcoming. I was unloved. Abandoned. Most painful of all, I was betrayed.

No one from the Foundation had asked me to leave, and yet I sensed that the stage was being set for my departure. I was scheduled to spend less and less time in the company of my fellow Founders and was exiled to the Foundation Faith Thrift Shop in Greenwich Village. A safe place to stow me, like so much unclaimed baggage. Out of sight, out of mind.

Oddly enough, it was in the Village that I found my niche. In a matter of weeks, I created a profitable business from what was previously a nondescript church thrift shop. It was the diversity of cultures and lifestyles that bound me to this artsy, eclectic neighborhood. No image-conscious Upper East Side chic. No decorum. No façade. I was quickly assimilated and became one more multicolor patch in the crazy quilt of humanity that makes life in the Village an ongoing piece of "performance art."

Success, as I soon found out, was not without its down

side. When the store had been a miserable failure no one wanted to be associated with it. Now that it was successful, everyone wanted a piece of the action. Rumblings and grumblings were heard in various sectors of the hierarchy. Being assigned to the store was now considered a perk, and therefore was to be given to someone with more seniority than I had.

Various members of the community were tried out, but my customers remained loyal. No one made as much money as I did. Perhaps because no one loved it there as much as I. Hierarchy may be hierarchy, but money is money, and in this instance, money won out. At least for the moment.

Despite my endless trials and tribulations, life went on. Weeks accumulated into months. Spring succumbed to summer. And so it came to pass that I found myself returning from the thrift shop to our communal living space in the company of a man named Joseph.

On the day of my encounter with Joseph, I arrived home hours after I was expected. My evening chores were still waiting for me. The drama of my day was merely an interesting postscript and, admittedly, the best excuse for tardiness that anyone in the community had ever heard. People were not entirely unsympathetic or unkind; they were just busy and tired.

I did not make it to bed until one A.M. I was emotionally and physically drained, to the point of total collapse. I prayed harder than I had ever prayed in my entire life. I was in such emotional and spiritual pain that I feared I could not bear it.

Two days after the incident with Joseph, as I was passing an electronics store, it caught my eye: a brand new TV set in the window, all plugged in and turned on. It was obviously supposed to make you want to run right in and buy it on the way home from work. The problem was that it had no picture. Just static. Mesmerized, I stood in front of it. In spite of myself, I could not move.

People on either side of me were also staring at the screen. Static, it seemed, did have a certain amount of mass appeal. Perhaps we could form a fan club. The man to my right began to communicate with whatever alien life form he had obviously spotted on the screen. He greeted it like a long-lost friend in an unidentifiable language of grunts and giggles. I scrapped the fan-club idea, deciding to quit while I was ahead.

Still, I remained rooted to the spot. There was something inherently comforting about static. None of the sensory demands of Technicolor. Nothing to see or hear or feel. None of the brooding ambience of black and white, with its angles and shadows and shades of gray. No film classics or nostalgic 1950s' Westerns or sitcoms. Static was just there, demanding nothing. And, in return, it gave nothing. Absolutely nothing at all. It was the electronic sign language of Purgatory. Neither here not there. Neither Heaven nor Hell.

The woman on my left poked me with her elbow and gestured with her head to the man on my right. "He's got static in his attic," she whispered while tapping the side of her head with her forefinger. She nudged me again with her elbow. This was obviously not a rhetorical observation on her part. It required a pithy reply so that I'd not be subjected to yet another elbow blow. Nudged to death.

The best I could come up with was "You're a poet and you just don't know it." I delivered this grade-school aphorism in a monotone voice and with a poker face, assuming it would bring a speedy, painless end to our camaraderie. Not so. She was so delighted that she scrunched up her forehead in search of another poetic gem. To my dismay, we were now co-conspirators.

Mercifully, I was rescued. My new-found friend spotted an acquaintance across the street, and, with a final wink of her eye and a jab with her elbow, she was off in hot pursuit of more convivial companionship.

Even in the midst of all that craziness, I couldn't seem to walk away from that damned TV set. Nor could I walk into the store to tell someone he really ought to change the channel. And then I had one of those amazing moments of clarity and enlightenment that all of us get from time to time. If we're lucky. Very lucky. It is a biblical, struck-by-lightning moment. A cosmic "thump upside your head" moment. Bells and whistles sounded. Internal worlds collided. I couldn't leave this TV set because it was a metaphor for exactly how I'd been living my life for the last four months, since my MS diagnosis.

As I stood there staring at the silent, static-filled screen, I began to realize that life is a lot like that TV set. When we're born, the Lord and the world give us a TV set with a hundred channels on it. Ninety-nine of those channels have something absolutely remarkable on them. One channel has static.

Everyone in the world has his or her own static channel. We can either sit in front of that channel for the rest of our lives, inventing reasons and justifications for our emotional inertia, or we can get up and change the channel.

My personal static channel had MS on it. If I lived my

life waiting to die, then I would not have lived at all. Joseph had taught me that life, even at its longest, is way too short. In the blink of an eye or the beat of a heart, we come and we go.

The fact that I was young gave me no ironclad guarantee on the body or the functioning of its parts. If I had a year, or a month, or even just a single day left in my life, I needed to get on with it, stop feeling sorry for myself, and make it count for something. I realized for the first time that the difference between *having* a disease and *being* one is far greater than a matter of semantics.

As for the ponderous philosophical question "Why me?," perhaps the answer was far simpler than I had suspected. Maybe the answer could be summed up in six letters. Two very simple words: "Why not?" Pithy. Succinct. And Zen. Very Zen.

Had I deliberately chosen this for myself, as the Foundation suggested? Maybe on some moot karmic level at which we all choose everything that happens every day of our lives. The problem is that we don't live on such a grandiose philosophical plane. We don't have access to the Divine Game Plan for the Universe or to the Great Karmic Scoreboard on a daily basis. We live in real time, in the here and now, and we can only hypothesize and speculate about the randomness and vagaries of world events as they unfold around us.

Why does anything happen in life? Why do babies die who have never even had a chance in life? What of wars and famines and hunger and death? Why did Joseph die on the bus in the embrace of a stranger rather than in the company of those who knew and loved him? If I could not come up with a plausible explanation for anything in the universe, why should my having MS make any more sense than anything else?

Maybe the only answer that makes any sense is that you get what you get in life; what you do with it is up to you. If I had to accept this unpredictable intruder known as MS as my lifetime companion, then let it be no idle interloper. Let it take on meaning and function in my life. Let it serve as my teacher. Let me learn from it whatever life lessons I'm meant to learn. And let me pass those lessons on to others. Let me become the ever-vigilant student so that in turn I may someday become the teacher. Let this be the purpose of my soul.

Standing in front of that TV set, I closed my eyes and tried to envision the future. Startled, I realized that it didn't include the Foundation. How could it? Its acceptance of me was contingent on my being a perfect specimen in its perfect world. Because no one in the community had ever become seriously ill, the members mistakenly assumed that they were the chosen ones, blessed and exempt from the randomness of life. I strongly suspected that time and circumstance would teach them otherwise.

True to my vision of the future, I was out of the Foundation within a year. It was a difficult parting of ways, with a totally predictable end scenario. While I was with them, I continued to make good money at the store in the Village. They, in turn, did not pay the rent on the store and instructed the landlord not to tell me. The first I knew of it was when a FOR RENT sign went up over the building. I was devastated. No one asked me to leave, but it was now made clear to me that I had no real place in the community.

It was the memory of Joseph that finally gave me the

courage to leave the Foundation and get on with my life. Of all the gifts and legacies he may have left behind, perhaps his greatest contribution was to a total stranger on the Sixth Avenue bus. In his death he taught me the meaning of life.

I left the Foundation a little older, a little sadder, and a little wiser. The night before I left, I held my very own name-changing ceremony. Once again, I chose the name Zoe, this time not as a reminder of any particular religious or philosophical affiliation. This time it was to serve as a living tribute to that basic, elemental force of life that will surge through my soul as long as there is breath in my body and animation in my spirit.

Circumstances will come and go. The world will change and so will I. I will adapt. I will endure. I will grow. And in every sense of the word, from moment to moment, I will be present for my life and I will truly be alive. For my name is Zoe. And Zoe means life.

Chapter 2

DEATH HAS A way of changing your life. In 1973, it was a man named Joseph on the Sixth Avenue bus. Fifteen years later the death is my own.

It is late afternoon in early winter, a bad time for MS, because it is the high season for respiratory infections, which, like so many other things, don't mix well with MS. Right now I'm fighting a particularly nasty case of bronchitis.

I'm working for Good Move Trucking, a Manhattan-based moving company that services the tristate area. We have an office on Twenty-third Street and Tenth Avenue, a small, windowless room with barely enough space for two desks set at right angles to each other and facing adjoining walls. I'm at one desk, and my boss, Andy, is talking on the phone at the other. He's the president; I'm the vice-president. Doug, a foreman, has come to the office to turn in his paperwork for the day's jobs, and now he's standing behind Andy, talking to me.

Doug is a big, strong guy with a second-degree black belt in Akido. We have this intense, brooding relationship that I have never quite been able to get a handle on. From the very first time I met him, I was absolutely sure I was supposed to know him, but I hadn't the vaguest notion why. It isn't about sex or mating or any of the man-woman stuff. It's way beyond that. There is a sense of mission, a sense of expectation that will not go away. The missing piece of the puzzle finally falls into place that afternoon as I sit in the windowless office, in downtown Manhattan, talking to Doug and fighting off bronchitis.

I am a great believer in natural remedies for the common ailments that pester and plague us, leaving us too sick to work but not sick enough, in good conscience, to stay home. I always take vitamin C for colds and bronchitis. I take gel caps now, but back then I took these big horse pills.

That day, I tossed one down without a thought, chased it with a slug of orange juice. More vitamin C. Toss. Slosh. Swallow. And all the while, I'm busy doing something else. Talking to Doug. Handling his paperwork. The mundane actions of a thousand afternoons. Autopilot.

But today all the pills don't go down. One catches in the top of my throat. My brain registers the snag and tells the throat it will be all right. Just swallow again. The throat obeys, and the pill gets stuck even worse. Alarm bells go off. I can't get a molecule of air. Nothing. This is the real thing. Sheer gut-wrenching terror sets in. Calm down. Think. You took CPR. Remember what to do. By the time I remember, I have neither the strength nor coordination to do it.

Andy, his back to me, is oblivious of what's happening. Doug at first sees only that I've stopped talking. Instinctively, I clutch my throat. I can't believe that I'm choking to death right here in front of him, with the worksheets on my desk and the January dusk falling on the city and Andy blithely talking on the phone behind me.

I don't know whether it's my sign language or the fact, as he tells me later, that I'm turning blue that propels Doug into action. But when his mind registers that I look like a Smurf, he realizes what's happening.

"Get the hell off the phone!" he yells at the clueless Andy. "She isn't breathing. She's dying!"

"It's OK, Zoe! I've got you!" are the last words I remember hearing from Doug.

Suddenly I am weightless. Lithe. Airborne. Doug. The pill. The office. No more. All gone. I am transported to a place called Bergen Lane. It is a residential street in a small town in Long Island, near where my father lives. I always thought that if I had a conscious choice of one final earthly moment to remember, one parting gift to take when exiting the planet, it would be the memory of Bergen Lane in the fall. Now it seems that's true.

Bergen Lane is all trees. A long, leaf-vaulted tunnel with a bit of sky and a patch of the Great South Bay, way off in the distance, at the very, very end. In the autumn, it is one of the most beautiful places I have ever seen. One big glorious burst of color. It's guaranteed to summon the leaf-kicking kid from the depths of even the Grinchiest of adults. And it is here that I journey in my final moments.

It takes no time at all. Concern, alarm, panic, and then the realization that I am dying. A thirty-second life review flashes before my eyes, and I think, "Oh, so this is it. This is how it all ends. Right here. Right now. How sad. How interesting. How amazing." I am at peace, floating above my body, looking down at Doug doing his best to get me to come back. I really have no feelings one way or another about how it all turns out. I'm neutral, ready to go either way. Doug makes the decision for me. He decides that I cannot and will not leave.

He whacks me on the back so hard that he leaves a hand

print that does not go away for several weeks. He grabs me in the Heimlich maneuver and repeats it several times, thrusting so hard that he bruises my sternum. He is enraged at me for having the audacity to terrify him like that and for daring to die right in front of him. He refuses to let it happen. Finally, the pill flies out of my mouth and straight across the room, but I'm still not breathing.

He begins CPR, refusing to allow me to leave. He drags me back. He forces me back into my body and demands that I live. I re-enter wtih a bone-rattling thud.

I am numb. And I am cold—so very, very cold. Doug is white and shaking. I tell him how cold I am, and he and Andy rub my hands, trying to get some warmth back into them.

Somehow we manage to get ourselves back together and finish the day's work. I go home and wake up the next day with a badly bruised sternum and the imprint of Doug's hand on my back. For the next two weeks, the marks and the pain are constant reminders of the incident. They are also graphic illustrations of the fact that the very core of my belief system is built on some pretty shaky presuppositions.

For I had figured out my death scenario fifteen years ago. I had multiple sclerosis, and some day, in some way, shape, or form, I would die from it. Maybe from complications brought on by an exacerbation, but more likely from serious injuries sustained in a fall. Some people are Frequent Flyers. Due to the chronic impairment of balance and loss of coordination that plague me, I'm what you might call a Frequent Faller. Too bad there are no bonus miles or travel privileges to be had. I'd be racking up those points. Big time.

Up until now it stood to reason that I had an iron-clad,

money-back guarantee: I'm going to die from MS; I am not going to die from something else. That would be impossible. My MS existed as a kind of health insurance policy, an inoculation against the random events in life. No need to worry about raging infernos, airplane crashes, or nuclear holocaust! My bases are covered. I can sit back and relax. It's the rest of the world that has to worry.

This has been the foundation of my life. And now this foundation has been kicked out from under me. So, then, what other assumptions are false? The vitamin C pill is the first domino. In its wake everything else comes crashing down.

When I was diagnosed, the common wisdom about MS was "Don't push yourself. Don't wear yourself down. Better safe than sorry." I played by the rules and discarded the notion that I could still have an active physical life. The most exercise I got was whatever it took for me to get from my apartment to the subway or bus and back again. I focused my energies on the spiritual, philosophical, and intellectual aspects of life. And it was a good life, one filled with good times, good friends, and good jobs.

Like everyone else on the planet, I had my low days and bleak moments. I learned that there was a certain amount of therapeutic value in throwing myself an occasional "pity party." A fifteen-minute interlude to hang a serious bottom lip and ponder my losses. But then it was time to implement the "TV-set theory of life": time to get up and change the channel.

Granted, there will always be those apocalyptic moments, unexpected and unwelcome, that catch me off guard. One in particular immediately comes to mind: seeing a young woman in her twenties, running up a flight of subway stairs in high-heeled shoes. That day she became the living embodiment of everything I have lost and will never have again. I cried all the way to work. By the end of the day, I was myself again. Sometimes to get through something you just have to go through it. And then you move on. A moment is just a moment. And a moment does not a lifetime make.

Each day has its own unique set of circumstances and choices and for better or for worse, we make up what we make up about them. I have the circumstance of MS in my life. I have made up a scenario of inevitable death and a sedentary lifestyle.

Now my whole metaphysical applecart has not just been upset; it's been overturned and thrown off a cliff. And all by a vitamin C pill. For if my basic assumption that I can die only from MS is obviously wrong, maybe it's also wrong to assume that I am incapable of living in the physical universe. Suddenly I am no longer willing to accept the limitations of a sedentary life, since they in no way guarantee a longer life. I can die from any damned thing at any given moment. Just like everyone else.

All these years I've been playing by the rules. If the rules don't work, who cares if I break them? Maybe there are no rules. What the hell, I'll make up a few of my own.

I begin to think of all the physical capabilities I have surrendered to MS over the years. In the name of self-preservation and life extension, I have become the ultimate spectator. It's time once again to become a player.

I decide that I want back everything I have given up to MS over the years, and I want it more than I have ever wanted anything in my life. And so I need to have a dream. One that will ask for everything I've got and still demand something more. One that will commemorate this moment for all time as the beginning of the second half of my new life.

I decide to run the New York City Marathon.

Oddly enough, I have never been a great marathon fan. I know who the major players are, and have greatly admired the perennial winner, Grete Waitz, over the years. But I never watch the race on TV and never read the papers the next morning to follow up on marathon stories. I guess the thing that fascinates me about the New York City Marathon is that people care enough to do it at all.

Somewhere in the back of my mind, I know that the marathon isn't just some random, last-minute idea that you get in your head. Hmmm, first Sunday in November. Marathon Sunday. Let's see . . . Go to the movies or run the marathon? What the hell, think I'll run the marathon. You can't do it without first backing yourself up with a whole program of conditioning and training.

I'll give it my absolute best. If I still don't make it, at least I will have learned some very important lessons about my boundaries and limitations. And if I do make it, I will have used every mental, spiritual, and physical resource at my disposal.

Ten years, nine marathons, and two world records later, all of this still remains true.

I MAKE A LIST of all my assets and all the reasons I believe I can do the marathon. Right at the top of the list? A highly developed sense of the absurd. The fact that I've decided to run the marathon is certainly proof of that. Second? A really good sense of humor. A handy asset in any situation and an essential companion in the rigors of marathon training. And last but not least, the ability to pursue and achieve a long-term goal. In other areas of my life, I have been able to envision a multitask outcome and formulate a plan to get there. I can see no reason why the marathon shouldn't be the same.

I make a second list of all my deficits. Potential liabilities that might thwart my plans or put a damper on my dreams. Limited eye-hand coordination. Unsteady gait. No strength or endurance.

Finally, I make a third list. It contains all the ways I can fix the items on the second list. I think up very tactile, down-to-earth strategies. I can play pinball to improve my eye-hand coordination. I can enroll in an Afro-Brazilian dance class to improve my gait. I will do weight-training to improve my stamina and endurance.

In the beginning, I have a picture of how it's going to be. I'm going to run the marathon without crutches, canes, or appliances of any kind. Just me in my trendy running outfit, sprinting across the finish line, like everyone else. This is my picture of the way a marathon finish line is supposed to look.

Way back when I was first diagnosed, I went out and ran just as fast as I could, with the wind on my face and the earth flying beneath me. I ran and I ran, on some level trying literally to outrun MS. I knew the odds were that I might lose that ability, and I wanted to remember with my heart and my senses what my brain and my legs might forget.

Fifteen years later, it is time to retrieve those sensory memories. If I am going to run a marathon, I will actually have to learn how to run again. I go out to a nearby park, put aside my cane, and try to run. My balance is a sublime cross between terrible and nonexistent. I can't run more than a couple of feet before I crash. Falling isn't good. I go out and buy hockey pads for my elbows and knees to cushion the impact of my falls. At best I look silly. At worst I look stupid.

Well-intentioned neighbors and friends walk up to me and say, "If that's the best you can do, why bother?" Initially, I am hurt, because I'm still at the point where I question myself. I am still holding fast to that picture of what a real runner is, gauging myself in terms of time and miles and appearances. And then one day, as I'm picking myself up off the pavement for what seems like the millionth time, it suddenly hits me. Yeah, this is the best I can do. And it's in Technicolor. Take it. Leave it. Like it or lump it. This is it, and it's good. No, it's not just good—it's fantastic!

In those first few weeks, I come to realize that looking stupid is an inherent component in the whole process of risk-taking and goal achievement. I think about how stupid Thomas Edison must have looked while he was trying a thousand different possibilities in the invention of the light bulb. I'll bet you anything that Madame Curie and Columbus had their sorry-looking moments, too.

If the worst I can do is look stupid, who cares? Will the "pretty" police come to my door and haul me in for offending someone's sensibilities? Probably not. The bottom line in life is: if you don't try, you can't fly. Looking stupid is not fatal, merely inconvenient. Inconvenience and I are old friends. It goes hand and hand with MS. We get along just fine.

But while stupid is one thing, futile is another. And it is becoming rapidly apparent that my picture of the marathon isn't going to work. If I persist, I am back on that static channel on the TV set. It's time to get up and change the channel. Again.

I realize that it isn't about whether I use appliances or not. It isn't about how I look. The object is to cross the finish line. As Malcolm X said, "By any means necessary." If my picture isn't going to work, I need a different picture. The problem is, I just don't know how to get it. I obviously need some help.

The logical place to start is the New York Road Runners Club, the sponsoring organization of the marathon. I call to explain my situation, and the woman on the phone says, "Oh, yeah, you want to talk to Dick Traum at Achilles."

"What's Achilles?"

"You know, it's the track club for . . . oh, for, you know . . ." and she can't seem to spit the word out. Finally, she hocks it up and coughs it through the line. It lands in my ear with an ugly splat: ". . . for handicapped runners."

This is not the word I expect or want to hear. Stunned, I call my friend Marsha and start to cry. "I'm not handicapped," I sob. "I don't want to go there and no one can make me." Looking stupid I am prepared to handle, but not being handicapped. I fear the word and the stereotype that seems to go along with it.

Marsha lets me get it all out and then says, "Go there. If you don't like it, you walk out. What are they going to do, handcuff you to a lamppost? Go there, and if they're a bunch of jerks sitting around and feeling sorry for themselves, walk away from it. But it just might be your ticket to the Marathon. You owe it to yourself to see what's there."

When I was first diagnosed with MS, support group meetings were not the goal-oriented, life-affirming events they have become in the 1990s. They were merely a bunch of people getting together to bitch and moan twice a month, pondering the parameters of their losses and waiting for life to get even worse. I barely survived two meetings and decided I would rather die staked out on a ant hill than go back to a third.

My only other contact with the disabled community was the occasional bit of spare change given to either an amputee or someone in a wheelchair panhandling in the streets. Obviously, this was not a subcullture I was anxious to be part of. It raised issues I had been avoiding for the last fifteen years. But if Dick Traum and this thing called "Achilles" are to be my entrance ticket into the Marathon, then for all intents and purposes, I'm choiceless.

I call Dick, and he tells me that the club meets for its biweekly workouts in the Road Runners headquarters on Eighty-ninth Street between Madison and Fifth Avenues in Manhattan. When people are assembled, they pair off with volunteers and head across the street to Central Park to do a bit of warm-up stretching and then put in some miles.

Even ten years after the fact, I can still remember my first night at Achilles. I strongly suspect that what is true of Achilles is—in some way, shape, or form—true of any nonprofit organization that attempts to meet the needs of such a broad spectrum subculture as the disabled. I am greeted at the door by two of the least socially adapted members. They have worn out both the patience and tolerance of the more mainstream members, and now lie in wait for newcomers.

One is a blind man who, presumably because of his blindness, can't tell the difference between my breast and a door knob. In his futile but enthusiastic attempt to open the door, I am groped. Not once but twice. Since I'm five feet seven and possess no vital organs that are door-knob level, I'm not buying any of it. The second time I warn him that I am spastic and have a hyper-knee reflex. Part of *my* disability. Therefore, it would behoove him to keep his groin area as far away as possible from my uncontrollable knee jerks, or suffer the consequences. His choice.

The other man is plagued by severe arthritis and is also obviously retarded. He immediately attempts to put his arm around my waist while demanding my home phone number so that we can go out on a date. He and the blind guy engage in a noisy argument about who saw me first and whose girlfriend I will be. Frantically, I look around for someone to rescue me. No heroes or heroines are forthcoming. Finally, I give up and tell the guy with arthritis my phone number. Well, not exactly my phone number, but *a* phone number. The number I give him is for New York City telephone information: 555–1212. He is appeased. And then somewhat perplexed. He whips out a tattered piece of paper with several women's names and phone numbers on it. "Jeez," he says, "you must live in a very big house. There sure are a lot of you with the same phone number." A cursory glance at his ad hoc address book confirms the fact that all his previous victims have given him exactly the same number: 555–1212. It appears I'm in good company.

I am just about ready to bolt for the street, glad to be escaping with my life and most of my sanity intact, when Dick Traum rescues me. He has a talent for spotting new people and understanding their initial fears and considerations. He rescues me from my two would-be suitors and introduces me to the main group, now assembled in the back room.

When I first walk into that room I am paralyzed with fear. There are blind people and people in wheelchairs. A veritable cornucopia of disabilities. I am slapped with the unreasonable but real fear that somehow all of these people have MS and—since being blind or in a wheelchair is my worst fear for myself—for one terrible moment I'm afraid I'll either throw up or pass out. Once again I am ready to make a mad dash for the street. But then I take a closer look around, and the moment passes. No one has two heads. No one is tap dancing naked on top of the table. As far as groups go, when you come right down to it, this one actually looks pretty normal.

When people ask me why I'm here, I tell them I'm going to run my first marathon in November. I have said the same words to friends, acquaintances, and co-workers, and nearly every one either laughed or acted incredulous. Here, for the first time, I meet not laughter but support. No one dismisses me. They welcome me and believe in me, because once, they too were new, frightened, and uncertain. Many of them have done multiple marathons, and they all started out right here. Perhaps my quest is not crazy after all.

On that first night, Dick himself takes me out and tells me a bit about Achilles, which came into existence in 1983. He is its president and founder. Dick is an above-the-knee amputee due to a freak auto accident, and Achilles is his way of supporting disabled individuals to participate in "mainstream" running events. Achilles encourages people to run for pure enjoyment, regardless of time, speed, or ability. "People doing the most they can" is the group's primary philosophy. The only prerequisites for joining Achilles are an interest in running and a willingness to try.

Over the years, Dick Traum's original vision has taken a form and direction that no one could have predicted in the early years. By 1997 Achilles has become a worldwide organization with 40 chapters in the United States and 111 chapters in 36 countries, including Cambodia, Poland, and South Africa. Achilles is no longer just an entry ticket to the New York City Marathon. It provides an impressive catalogue of programs as diversified as its membership: running for the blind, free eye surgery, wheelchair basketball, specialized running programs for disabled children. And the list goes on. One man's vision come full cycle. One man's dream gone global.

On that first night, back in 1988, we do a half-mile—a quarter-mile out and back—together in the park, he on his prosthesis and I with a cane. I would have gone farther if left to my own devices, but Dick was wise enough to know that I would try to do too much. He held me to the half-mile, and at the end of it I am really beat. Although it's not a huge distance, it's a start: the first installment toward the base I will need ten months from now to run my first marathon.

At the end of the night, Dick asks me, "What are you feeling right now?"

I am silent, my thoughts in turmoil. I am not going to open up to a stranger. What would I say? That this is partly a freak show and I'm scared to death and I don't know if I even belong here? He waits and then says, "If you can talk about what you're feeling, you'll be back. If you can't, you never will."

I realize that he's right, and I understand that I've been functioning according to a stereotype of what I think *disabled* is. But I don't have to be that stereotype of disabled any more than I am a "stereotypical" woman or a "stereotypical" forty-year-old. If I've refused to buy into that on other levels, why should this be the exception? And so I decide, what the hell, if I'm going to be disabled, then I'm going to be disabled the way no one has ever been disabled before. I am going to bring *my* essence and *my* sense of style and color to it. If, by joining Achilles, I have joined this subculture, why not do it right?

Twice a week, on Tuesdays and Saturdays, I go to Achilles meetings. On the other days I train by myself in Stuyvesant Park. At Achilles, I meet other members and learn about their lives and how they became disabled. Every disability you can possibly imagine is represented in Achilles—and a few you can't. What a fluke life is sometimes. For example, there is the person in the wheelchair who left his house in the morning to go off to work, got hit by a drunken driver, and woke up paralyzed. And then he went on. Not only did he go on, he's done it big time. He's learned new skills, reinvented himself. So, instead of finding a bunch of people sitting around feeling sorry for themselves, moaning about their losses, I find a remarkable group of people. Not every one of them; not by any means. We're the same as any subculture that way. We've got our share of winners and losers. But good and bad, we are people who have been forced by life to kick it up a notch. Outsiders see us as heroic or courageous. I look at myself as being pragmatic, doing what I have to do to live the best life that I possibly can.

My first race is a 5K Road Runners race in Central Park in the dead of winter. The course is all ice, a surface on which I am not at all good. I have these James Bond kind of steel claws on my crutches to help give me a grip, but at best, it's a shaky proposition. Before the race begins, I do what every runner does before a race: go to the bathroom. They have a bunch of portable johns around the starting area. No matter how many there are, there are never quite enough, and there's always a big line in front of each one.

This is my first time in a portable john. Maneuvering in close spaces has never been my forte to start with. To complicate matters, the floor is covered with ice. The claw tips on my crutches keep sliding, and the next thing I know, the crutches fly out from under me and I fall into the toilet bowl. My butt promptly freezes to the seat. At first, I'm really pissed off, because, let's face it, no one wants to be frozen to a toilet seat. I'm struggling back and forth, trying to get a grip with the crutches, and the whole john is rocking back and forth.

As the absurdity of the situation hits me, I begin to laugh hysterically. The john is rocking back and forth so vehemently that it's in imminent danger of tipping over. My butt is still frozen to the seat. And on top of that, there must be a hundred people lined up outside, watching the rocking john and making up all kinds of scenarios, most of them far more interesting and erotic than what is actually happening.

I finally pry myself up, pull my clothes back on, and emerge, victorious over the evil clutches of the portable john. It's the dumbstruck, amazed look on the faces of the waiting runners that sets me off again into peals of helpless laughter. They keep looking over my shoulder, waiting for my mythical partner to emerge. By silent group consensus, the now vacant john remains unoccupied.

I don't bother feeling stupid. I'm way past that. Stupid was when I couldn't get up the first time. After that, I was so grateful that the damned thing didn't tip over, everything else was a bonus. Anyway, how can you stay mad about anything so funny?

I go out buoyed by my victory in "The Battle of the Portable john." That sense of absurdity carries me through the race as I pick my way across the ice with my James Bond claw tips, laughing and having a great time all the way. I finish the three miles in a little over two hours. Dead last. I get a T-shirt for my outside and euphoric feeling for my inside. I can do this. I can be a runner.

I enter every race that Road Runners sponsors. Building. Building. Building. In between races and training, I play pinball and take Afro-Brazilian dance classes. I find the first few classes intimidating, because there are so many complicated steps involved. Initially, the teacher is worried that I'm not getting all the steps. I go to her after class and tell her that I'm getting the steps all right. I just can't do them. I tell her that when it's a clear-cut matter of choreography, I'll move to the side so as not to screw everyone else up. The very end of the class is my favorite part. We have this circle where people spontaneously jump into the middle and do their own thing. I'm a real super star at this, because I know that you dance as much with your heart and your spirit as you do with your legs. Maybe even more so. Anyway, the bottom line is that the dance classes help me get some great rhythmic pelvic movement back. And this can definitely come in handy in other nonrunning related aspects of life. Enough said.

Early on, my friends start kidding me about my new avocation. At work, they start calling me Grete. After Grete Waitz, the queen of the New York City Marathon, and for my money the greatest marathoner ever, man or woman. They call me Grete so much, that it kind of becomes my nickname, and some of our customers think it's my real name. The joke blooms when my co-workers start telling people that, on weekends, I rent myself out as a Grete Waitz look-alike. They ask me how I will ever keep spectators from mistaking me for Grete during the marathon. Easy, I tell them. I'll just have to carry a sign saying, "I'm not Grete."

About the same time, my friends start wondering how I will dress for the marathon. Knowing me, they're betting on how many different colors I can tastefully combine in my marathon outfit. As luck would have it, I have a big white shawl, trimmed with a fringe of every color in the rainbow. And even a few that aren't. It's a blank, triangular canvas, begging to be painted on.

I also have Flash, a stuffed turtle I found in one of those funky East Village stores I'm inordinately fond of. If I were a turtle, I'd look just like Flash. He's got big blue eyes, gigantic sneaker-clad feet, and stereo headphones that are perpetually glued to his head. I name him "Flash the Miracle Racing Turtle." He becomes my mascot. A cartoonish personification of what I'm well on my way to becoming. The Miracle Racing Turtle.

I take Flash and the shawl to the Unique Clothing store on Broadway in Manhattan. They have a whole bunch of graffiti artists there who can hand-paint T-shirts—or shawls. I watch them work for a while and then pick the artist who I think will do the best job. When I tell him the whole story about how this is my first marathon and why it means so much to me, he feels he's become part of a great adventure.

I show him the stuffed turtle and tell him that I want Flash duplicated bigger than life on the shawl. I also tell him about my friends teasing me that no one will be able to tell me apart from Grete Waitz in the marathon. I now have the perfect solution. I want him to inscribe the legend I'M NOT GRETE. I'M FLASH FROM THE ACHILLES TRACK CLUB on the shawl in big bold letters. The whole thing is going to cost about ten dollars tops.

An hour later, I come back to pick up my shawl. The artwork is just great. Flash has never looked better. But English is not the artist's primary language, and when he gets done with it, it reads ACHILLED TRACK CLUB. He feels really terrible about it, but he's done such a great job, I can't possibly be angry at him. "Trust me," I tell him. "When I get done running, I will be 'Achilled.' And someday, somewhere, you will see this shawl again and you'll say, 'I painted that.' So know that this is your contribution to my life."

I often wonder where that artist has gone and whether he has ever recognized the often photographed Flash and the infamous ACHILLED TRACK CLUB inscribed for all time on the back of that shawl, as his special creation.

I also buy and wear a pair of big rhinestone earrings I get for a couple of bucks in an antique store. I tell people I wear them to blind bikers, because bike riders are always a problem for runners in the park. (The bike riders, of course, see it the other way around.) And then there is that wonderful pewter pin that I find at a jewelry stand on Broadway and Eighth Street. When I see it I think, "God, that's my perfect self." It's a woman with billowing hair dotted with rhinestones. She's the real me. The inner Zoe.

So now my marathon outfit is all together, give or take a couple of last-minute accessories. All I need is to continue training and successfully complete a half-marathon. I fervently hope I'm up to it.

The big test for every Achilles athlete is the summer half-marathon—thirteen miles of hot pavement. It is your entry ticket to the marathon. There was a good reason for this qualifying race back when Achilles and the idea of disabled people doing marathons was new. If anything were to happen to a disabled athlete because the athlete was unfit to run, that would be the end of Achilles.

The race is in Central Park in August, another bad time for MS, with the heat and humidity at an all-time high. I think it will be OK—at least I can't get stuck to a toilet seat. But you never know until you're out there doing it. Thirteen point one miles is twice as long as my previous longest race—10K, or six point two miles. Besides the ordinary prerace jitters, I am nervous because I genuinely don't know if everything I've done is going to be enough. That's a risk you take in any new enterprise.

I start several hours before the main body, along with other Achilles runners who are expected to take longer than average to complete the course. My volunteer, Sue, will remain at my side for the entire run, no matter how long it takes. The race is tough but uneventful till the final stages. Some of the slower runners in the main pack are still catching and passing me. One of them, a middle-aged man, is about to pass me when he collapses in his tracks. Runners do all kinds of crazy things, and this man, who knows he has a heart condition, has been running with angina, taking nitroglycerine pills along the way but not stopping. Until he catches up to me, when he goes into cardiac arrest. It is Joseph all over again in the sticky New York summer, only this time he is not alone. He has friends with him, and they are screaming at him not to die. And he has me. I know CPR now, and I drop down on the pavement, ready to start to work on him.

Before I can do much, a doctor and a nurse, who as luck would have it are running right behind him, take over. This day, he is blessed. I guess I am too. They save his life, and I'll find out later that he underwent a multiple bypass, pulled through, and eventually returned to running.

When I am sure he is taken care of, I pick myself up and continue on the final stretch of the course. My knees and elbows are scraped and bleeding. I look like a five-year-old who's had a rough day on the playground. I finish that way, looking pretty yucky. I'm not sorry I stopped. I'm not sorry I got involved. It amazes me that people can turn their heads and walk away from so many things in life. Sometimes I've got to admit that I wish I could too. But I never can. I really get caught up in the moment.

By the time Sue and I get to the finish line, nine hours or so after the start, there is no finish line. No one handing out medals, T-shirts, or cups of Gatorade. I don't mind, for I've won the biggest and best prize of all: I have proved myself. I have what it takes. I have officially qualified as an Achilles Track Club entrant in the upcoming 1988 New York City Marathon.

This half-marathon also serves as a good indicator of what I can expect from a full marathon. It's a welcome reassurance that I'm not going to die, go blind, or end up in a nursing home a week later. What a tremendous relief.

Five weeks until Marathon Sunday, I lose my volunteer, Sue. She is a magazine editor and has just found out that, because it's a presidential election year, she will be required to work for at least part of the day. For many runners like me, there is no marathon without a volunteer. Ideally, it's not a casual partnership thrown together the day of the race, especially since I'm going to spend nearly twenty hours with this person. My volunteer not only helps carry changes of clothing and supplies, but she also has to know me well enough to realize when I'm pushing too hard, when I need rest stops, and when I should take a drink of water. After the half-marathon, Sue has a really good handle on all of this. And now it appears that I'm back at square one. It's almost like a prom date: you don't want to be scrambling late for one and you don't want to replace the one you have at the very last minute. I have trained for this event all year, and now I'll simply have to take what is left over.

It never dawns on me that Hester might be available. In my eyes, she is such a choice volunteer that it's incomprehensible that she hasn't already committed to volunteer for someone else. We've become friendly at Achilles meetings. Hester is from New Jersey and comes with her daughter, Maude, who is a wheelchair athlete. When Maude goes out with her volunteer, Hester frequently goes out with me. We are part of a larger group of women, each around forty. Some of the younger members affectionately refer to us as the Crones, because we are comparatively so much older than everyone else. Be that as it may, the laughter that emanates from our group can be heard loud and clear on any given Tuesday night as it echoes through the park.

When Hester learns of my predicament, much to my relief and total amazement she offers to be my volunteer. The idea of spending twenty hours or so on the road doesn't faze her a bit.

We don't really know each other all that well, don't know how much we have in common, or how strong the bonds between us will grow. She is black and I am white, a minor detail to which many will attach much meaning over the years. As for us, we rarely if ever think about it. We will become friends in the way that grown-up women who have been around the planet a few times can be friends. Sharing knowledge, ideas, and accumulated wisdom. We will become friends in the way that teenage girls can be friends, laughing, giggling, and making horrible, tasteless jokes. Ultimately, we will become sisters, bound together for all time by the strength of a common dream. In the years that follow, we will spend well over two hundred hours on the road together, cross nine finish lines, and set two world records. But we have no way of knowing any of this on that night when Hester first offers her services as my volunteer.

Five weeks later, after ten months of rigorous training, we finally make it to the starting line. And so, on that cold November morning back in 1988, begins what will become the journey of a lifetime. Our first New York City Marathon.

CHAPTER 3

No one can prepare you for what it's like to see the sun come up on the Verrazano Narrows Bridge. There's just you and a great red-and-orange ball boiling out of the Atlantic Ocean, and that bridge soaring into the sky. Stretching into the infinite.

It is one of the most awesome sights I have ever seen. To this day, I can't see it and not get choked up. For me, the bridge has always been a siren song. It teases. It beckons. "Come hither. Here I am. I've got your day. Come get it."

But when I was preparing for my first marathon, I had never seen the bridge, never been to Staten Island, never been to most of the places on the marathon route. That's typical of New Yorkers. We tend to be very territorial. Most of us pick a part of the city and make it our own. Mine is the East Village. But today, the entire city will be mine.

I've been up since three A.M. and haven't had much sleep. Too excited. Too many thoughts about what is to come. Pre-race jitters. There's so much to do. Sandwiches to make. Layers of clothing to pack. Copies of the marathon map. And Advil, always Advil.

The journey really starts at the New York Public Library on Forty-second Street and Madison Avenue. The brigade of buses that take the thousands of runners to the starting line leaves from here. The first one is filled with Achilles athletes, who will need extra time to complete the race. The ride to the bridge goes quickly in the dark and nearly deserted streets. The city may never sleep, but at this hour it's at least heavily napping.

We disembark at the bridge, on an embankment above the ordered, military sprawl of Fort Wadsworth. Hester and Sue, my two volunteers, are at my side. Sue will need to leave after the first five miles to go to work, but she'll return later in the evening. I scan the crowd for familiar faces. All the people who work with me at Good Move have promised to show up. None of them have. There is a lesson here. People make commitments with good intentions, but then real life shows up—and they don't. It's not personal, but it still hurts.

I have a definite picture of what the marathon is going to be like. I'm certain that it's going to be this straight-line, go-get-'em, don't-even-stop-for-a-cup-of-tea thing. It's like my original picture of the act of running. I assume I'll do it the same way everyone else does.

But none of this is what I've imagined. The first shock comes just five or ten minutes before six A.M., when they call us to the starting line. We are an eclectic crew, on crutches or artificial limbs, in wheelchairs, some going backward in wheelchairs because that is the only way they can go. Each of us has one volunteer or more.

In the gathering light, we walk out into the upper roadway, closed now to traffic. I look up and out at that enormous expanse of bridge and think, "Dear Lord, have I bitten off more than I can chew?"

Till now, I had no idea of the vastness of what I've undertaken, and this awesome bridge, a mile across, has slugged me right in the gut. It's almost like Dorothy's vision of the Emerald City, something huge and magical. When we cross it, we'll find ourselves singing, "Follow the Yellow Brick Road." I can't *not* sing it, because for me that's what the bridge is, and that's what the marathon is. It's Dorothy. It's Oz. It's the Lion. It's the Tin Man. It's Munchkins. It's witches falling from the sky. It's all of it, every single bit of it. And it's more. A cross between *The Muppets Do Manhattan* and a female version of Indiana Jones, with a bit of *Pee-Wee's Big Adventure* thrown in for good measure.

As I stand there on that bridge for the first time on that cold November morning, I suddenly realize, "Dorothy, we're not in Kansas anymore."

One of the things that thrills me every year is the knowledge that, even as we're setting out on our own adventure, thirty thousand people are waking up and getting on the buses. They are en route to the bridge, for their own great adventures. In the course of the day, however briefly, many of our paths will cross.

There is a last lecture from an Achilles running coach. Pace yourselves. Drink plenty of fluids. Don't overheat. She gives us an emergency phone number—just in case. A reminder that this is serious business. Six A.M. Runners ready. The starting horn is sounded. We're off, pushing, wheeling, and skittering, each of us after our own fashion.

This is where our MGM production begins. I dance on the gratings and sing silly songs. The sun is climbing out of the water as we climb to the crest of the bridge. I will learn over the years to judge the day by the bridge. On a good day, you can see from New Jersey to the ends of the earth. You can see the rain coming from the West and judge at what time it will arrive and where we'll be on the course. The bridge is a barometer. The bridge is a promise. A metaphor for what the day will be.

If we had known that first year, we might have been prepared for what would happen later, when the day was used up, the sun was gone, and our dance had become a forced march. But we didn't know, and we merely listened with amusement when a track club official on a bicycle rode up to us on the bridge and started lecturing about how we were going to go into oxygen deficit because we were laughing so hard. Over the years, this will become a part of our ritual on the bridge as well. We'll remember that moment and laugh again, oxygen be damned.

The crest of the bridge is nearly three hundred feet above the water, the highest point on the entire marathon route. From there it's a long downhill into Brooklyn. It takes at least a half-hour to get all the way across. When we arrive on the far shore, I turn and bow to the bridge in homage.

I have the map of the race route that every runner gets. It is the same map that I will take every year and that I carry still. Mainly, we are guided by the blue line painted on the streets. We are alone in Brooklyn, just after dawn. It will be several miles and hours before spectators start to come out, more than four hours before the main pack of runners will catch up to us.

By the second mile, it becomes apparent that we are seriously overequipped. We are outfitted as if we are afraid of becoming the Donner Party; we have enough provisions to last us forever. We don't even think that there are stores along the route where we could buy things. A note for the future: travel lighter. The things you really need are clothes. The rest you can make up as you go along.

WHEN WE START, we have no idea that we'll ever have to stop. It soon becomes apparent that that's not going to work: I'm going to need more water than I can carry; there will have to be food stops, and bathroom stops, and I will need to sit down and rest from time to time if I am going to make it.

It goes back to when I began to train. I thought I could run without appliances. That didn't work. And so I began to ask some pertinent questions. What's my goal? What's my outcome? I must remove everything that stands in the way of achieving that outcome. If eating, drinking, and making the occasional rest stop are what's going to get me to the finish line, then it's time to scrap Plan A and get with Plan B.

So begins a day at the Improv. Many of the places we stop at this year, we will stop at every year. They will become part of our history and we of theirs. I take breaks at least every four miles, simply because I have to. At Mile 3 we are dying from low blood sugar, and we stop for a quick cup of coffee. The jolt of caffeine does us a world of good. About Mile 8, there's Sal and Sarah's Pizza place in Brooklyn. We use the bathroom there and have a slice of pizza. At Christina's in Brooklyn, we grab a fast cup of chicken soup. A little liquid fortification before we hit the windswept Pulaski Bridge and the halfway point of the marathon. Then, just before the Fifty-ninth Street Bridge, we stop at the Good Sports Bar in Long Island City. Another needed bathroom break and a glass of orange juice. Later, everyone there will know us, and each year they'll sit in the bar checking the time, debating whether we should be there yet. Nice people.

Then it's a five-mile haul through Long Island City and across the Queensboro Bridge to First Avenue and Seventy-ninth Street for our dinner stop at the Cafe 79. In the South Bronx there's a McDonald's. Another bathroom break. Another caffeine fix. In Harlem, in the middle of the night, there's an after-hours bar with a peephole in the locked door. Sometimes the friendliest, most obliging people can be found in the most unlikely setting.

But today we have been to none of these places yet; don't really know where the blue line will lead us. We just follow it for those first few miles, make that first coffee stop, put one foot in front of the other, willing and eager to go wherever the day and the blue line will take us.

Almost half of the New York City Marathon is run in Brooklyn. It is where we spend all our daylight hours and the only borough in which we have any contact with the crowd. By the time we get to Queens and Manhattan, the spectators have gone home, the medical tents and the water stops have folded up and departed, and the streets will have reopened to traffic. The marathon will be an official fait accompli, except, of course, for those of us who are still out there running it.

I love Brooklyn in the same way and for the same reasons that I love Manhattan. I love the spontaneity and generosity of its people. I love the diversity of their cultures and their ability to blend and weave the differences into a tapestry of infinite sights, smells, tastes, and sounds. In Brooklyn, as in the rest of the city, the marathon is celebrated as if it were a national holiday. It is the borough of hugs and handshakes. There is nothing that we could need or hope for that is not freely offered and joyfully given.

"Hey, wanna use our bathroom?"

"Wanna stay for lunch?"

"Wanna date my brother?"

"Lookin' good, girl! You can do it. Trust me, I know you can!"

There is a kind of energy here I don't feel in quite the same way in other parts of the city. It is raw and often fragmented, but always compelling. If it was harnessed and directed, I know it would be a force to be reckoned with in the battle against the drugs, homelessness, and poverty that plague so many of its neighborhoods. Brooklyn, to me, is a borough of possibilities.

The people of Brooklyn never ask me why I'm doing this; there are no great philosophical discussions of the spiritual or social ramifications of sports for the disabled. People know why I'm here. Like so many of them, I'm living my life against the odds. I'm doing what I can and doing what I must. Just to survive. A block at a time, with their unwavering enthusiasm and support, I'm achieving a dream that's bigger than me. And though we live a river, a borough, and a lifestyle apart, these people are my neighbors.

On Fourth Avenue, around the fourth or fifth mile, we approach a young mother with her newborn baby in a top-of-the-line carriage. She's waving a giant homemade sign that says, GO, ACHILLES! GO!

We are still alone on the course, the great tide of runners somewhere behind us. They will not be here for a while, and the curbs are not yet lined with spectators. The fans who are early really stand out, and when you see someone holding a sign like that, you assume she is looking for a specific runner. We slow down to ask who she knows in Achilles.

She points to her brand-new baby in the carriage. "I know my daughter," she says.

We are blown off the planet. She introduces us to her daughter, Meena. She looks as if she might have Down syndrome, but we don't ask and the mother doesn't volunteer any information. It is enough to know that Meena was born with a severe disability and that her mother knows it.

Instead of being crushed, this mother is full of hopes and plans for Meena. "I want you to know who we are," she says. "Ten years down the road, we're going to need you to be there for us. My daughter is seriously disabled. Who knows? Maybe some day she'll want to run a marathon. I'll tell her all about you folks at Achilles, and she'll know she's not alone. Your being out here today paves the road for her being out here in the future."

Meena's mom makes me realize that we see parents with disabled children and invent our own realities; we tend to think that they lead lives of quiet desperation. But Meena's mom shows us this is just not true. She is a shining reminder that by and large people lead absolutely remarkable lives of courage, humor, and compassion. Her love and dedication to her daughter are total and unconditional. Instead of limitations, she sees possibilities. She doesn't know what they will be, but she wants her foot in the door way ahead of time.

"I'm going to keep on showing up year after year for as long as it takes," she tells us. We thank her for her support and tell her that we'll remember. It seems inadequate, but there are no other words. We push on through the next few miles in total silence, each of us lost in our own thoughts and introspections.

And the next year, she will be there again. With the same sign and a different, bigger carriage. Again we'll stop and talk and she'll tell us of her hopes for Meena. She'll become part of our journey, part of the passion play that renews itself annually along the blue line.

The next year she'll be there again, the carriage growing larger with Meena, her enthusiasm and hopes undiminished. But the fourth year, she won't be at her familiar station. We'll never see her again.

I wonder what happened to them. Maybe they moved. Maybe Meena died. All things are possible. I wonder about all the people who became part of our journey and then disappeared. How many of the gang kids we've befriended in the Bronx will still be alive five years later? Will any of the broken lives we encounter ever be mended?

We are free to assume any reality. I choose to believe the best. It is the lesson of Meena and her mom, the lesson of choosing courage and optimism instead of quiet desperation.

A couple of miles and hours down the road, the crowds begin to assemble, everyone angling to get a good glimpse of the lead runners as they pass. Some people wait with encouraging signs and banners supporting friends or family who are running the race.

Suddenly, a man reaches out from the crowd and grabs my arm. He may be no older than I am, but drugs and alcohol have taken a horrible toll, aging him well beyond his years. Tears are streaming down his face. He looks at me and says, "When you cross that finish line—whether it's today, tonight, or tomorrow—think of me. Take some part of me over that line. Cross that line for me, too. 'Cause you're all I've really got."

That year and every year, I do think of him when I cross the line. And some part of him does go with me. I wish for him a dream that's worthy of his time and devotion. I wish for him a plan to implement that dream. And I wish him a life that is free from the addictions that enslave him.

ACHILLES TOLD US that, at some point in the race, the lead pack of elite runners and then the main mass—a great river of pounding feet and sweating flesh—will catch up and pass us by. We've been instructed to move to the right of the course, to let them pass and to avoid injury.

That first year, it happens around Mile 9. A flurry of helicopters and motorcycles. Fred Lebow, the race director, in his Mercedes convertible. Trucks full of photographers and reporters. We step up on the curb and turn to watch the male leaders of the pack pass us by. I am in awe of their beauty and grace. Could it be that their feet never really touch the ground, or is that just my heightened perception of them? I feel their light, their heat, and their energy. I am deeply touched. I see the winning moment pregnant in their faces, just as it will be on my face, many miles and many hours down the road. Right now, for this moment in time, the only real difference between us is a matter of pace and stride.

With a conscious act of choice, I bridge that difference. I close that gap. I let my heart and imagination run with the pack. I am wild and I am free. I am a metaphysical study in speed and light, with all parts perfect and coordinated. Unencumbered and unstoppable in spirit, I run the miracle mile. Even knowing that this fantasy voyage is the closest I will ever come to running a five-minute mile does not diminish the euphoria. I have just been passed by some of the best in the business. They are like fine, beautiful animals. Almost in flight. I am moved to tears. I am inspired.

The pack disappears quickly, and there is a gap before the next pack comes. At first the runners are sparse, still running relatively free. It is another visceral thrill when the lead women arrive. Grete Waitz, unstoppable, unmatchable, all grace and power and beauty, is the undisputed front runner. I stand aside and cheer her on. Finally, maybe ten minutes after the first runners, there is an approaching thunder we can hear and feel. The entire sidewalk shakes—and twenty thousand more people show up on the course.

In no way am I prepared for the intensity of feeling that this massive onslaught of mainstream runners unleashes in me. It is a profoundly emotional moment. All these dreams, all this energy. Hooked into one system, one moment, one goal.

In a moment or two, we pick up our backpacks and hit the road again. I am buoyant. I am renewed. This is one of the high points of the day for me. The moment when I have it all. I have the thrill of being a spectator and the heady rush of being a participant. The best part of all is that I've experienced both simultaneously.

Several miles down the road, still in Brooklyn, we see the first runners who have finished the race getting out of the subways and going back home. They are wrapped in their shiny Mylar blankets, the women with roses and all of them with their medals around their necks. We stop them, eager to see what the finisher's medal looks like. We talk. We swap training stories. We exchange hugs and kisses.

This is another part of my outcome process, because now I can see the medal. It's real to me. I know what it looks like. And best of all, I know that at journey's end I'll have my very own.

Brooklyn invariably comes to an end, although some years I must admit that I think it never will, since the route encompasses almost twelve miles. And so we pass another mile marker, pick up a whole bunch of friends, and enter another borough and the adventure goes on.

There is still no evidence of any of my co-workers from Good Move. I check my answering machine. No inquiries as to how and where we are. No excuses as to why no one has kept his word. Not even a solitary message of support or encouragement. In spite of myself, I am deeply disappointed.

We trudge on through the two miles of deserted factory district in Long Island City. During the years that we are not fortunate enough to have friends along, that stretch of the marathon course can be both boring and annoying. As the years have gone by and I have become incrementally slower, the darkness comes earlier on the route. Compounded by the desolation, these miles require our undivided attention. Anyone or anything could be lurking in the deserted parking lots or abandoned warehouses we pass along the way.

Long Island City comes to a merciful end, and we cross the East River on the pedestrian walkway of the Queensboro Bridge. The open grating of the walkway is the exact size to swallow up a crutch tip. It is a torturous crossing, one in which every step must be plotted, planned, considered, and executed. Off the bridge, then, up endless First Avenue. A quick dinner stop at Mile 17 at the Cafe 79, and then it's back to First Avenue and over the Willis Avenue Bridge into the Bronx. After a short stretch in the South Bronx, we cross the final bridge of the marathon course, the Madison Avenue Bridge, which brings us back across the Harlem River into Manhattan. We are on Fifth Avenue, the axis of Manhattan. Dead smack in the middle of Harlem.

You can see that once this was a fine neighborhood. Once. Now it's an avenue of despair and devastation. The once handsome apartments and brownstones are wrecked and abandoned, and yet lights glow from within where the crackheads are buying rock and smoking it and the homeless are staking out potential winter living quarters. It's a parallel universe, one in which everything is turned inside out, where good is transmuted into evil, hope into despair. This is the roughest part of the city, the netherworld.

I am devastated by what I see, overwhelmed by the aura of decay and despair. The image will haunt me for that entire first year. I am used to going wherever I want in life. I had looked at the map of the race before I began, but the dotted line of the route had no meaning for me. It didn't dawn on me that there might be consequences to being somewhere like this long after dark. And it's scary.

And this is where, around Mile 23, that I hit my wall, that mythical and yet very real structure every marathoner knows so well. It is the distance runner's worst nightmare. To paraphrase Robert Frost: Something there is in a man that does not love a wall. Well, let me tell ya, Bobby baby, here's something in a woman that ain't real fond of it either.

My feet hire a lawyer and bring suit against my shoes, citing harassment and unlawful imprisonment. They want out. RIGHT NOW.

I feel kind of like the Starship *Enterprise* when Captain Kirk asks for Scotty's damage report after a Klingon attack, and Scotty sighs in deep despair. "Aye, Captain. She'll never make warp speed again."

Maybe you're right, Scotty, at least for tonight. But you can bet your dilithium crystals I've still got impulse power. All life support systems are still functioning, and I can limp my way home.

For me, hitting the wall is an opportunity to see what's on the other side of where I usually give up in life. It's a chance to go deep inside myself and really appreciate all that I usually take for granted. It's a moment to acknowledge that source, that well-spring of pure spirit that can pursue a dream far beyond the boundaries of rhyme or reason. It's a time to say thank you for how far we've come. It's a time to ask for blessings on the last few remaining miles.

For now, the mechanics of locomotion have become more complicated. My left side is my weaker side, and as I go deeper into my reserves, my left leg sometimes simply quits on me. A simple curb can become Mount Everest, nearly unscalable.

Those are the times when Hester finds a park bench, and I flop down. I close my eyes and visualize my misfiring nerves as macramé knots, and then, one by one, I untie them. Or I'll see myself as an electrical plant, where the wiring starts way up on top, and when it gets to the bottom, it's connected to the wrong outlet. Sometimes I just visualize disconnecting all the wires and then reconnecting them one by one. Each time I reconnect a wire, I visualize the energy moving along the proper path.

Sometimes I fill my body with light or color or sound. I

may visualize the energy as a colored fluid that I can hear and watch flow. It depends on the mood I'm in. Sometimes, some things work better than others. And sometimes I just make it up as I go along. Whatever gets me through the night.

I find out that first year that it's really important not to get angry with my body. The way I look at it is that I'm basically asking it for a favor. A really BIG favor. Hey, body, would you mind staying awake, alert, and in perpetual motion for more than twenty-four hours? If someone asked that kind of favor from me, they'd better ask nicely. Very nicely.

And so I engage in a dialogue. Hey, how ya doin', legs? Where are we here, feet? What do you think, hands? And eventually I can visualize things running again, more or less smoothly.

I am sitting on the steps of a small church, taking a break, reconnecting the wires. The damage reports are in. All systems are present and accounted for. As far as I can tell, no wheelchair or Seeing Eye dog in my immediate future. I'm spastic. I'm tired and I'm sore. So what else is new? My ten months of rigorous training have really paid off. There's nothing wrong with me that a hot bath, a good night's sleep, and a couple of bottles of Advil won't cure.

As I sit there, a car pulls up and its door swings open. It is an official from Achilles who has come out on the course to tell us something. She doesn't look at me, only at Hester. Though her words are clear, her message is incomprehensible to us.

"You've had enough. It's time for you to go home."

I am devastated, but I'm not getting in the car, and neither is Hester or anyone else from my crew. I feel betrayed.

The fact that someone could ask me to give up a dream that has taken everything I've had to give, over a period of eleven months, simply because I've become an inconvenience is crushing. It goes right to that secret place in my heart where I hold the absence of the people from Good Move who had promised to be there for me and then turned into chicken liver at the last minute.

She sees that we're not being obedient and gets out of the car. I am flabbergasted. It isn't as if no one knew we were still out here. We called an hour or two ago, just to let them know we were OK and would finish. No one had checked in on us the entire day or night. Now suddenly we have to quit?

She walks up to me, puts a patronizing arm around my shoulder, and gives me a pat on the back. It feels like something from a Mafia movie: the bad guy puts his arm around you just to distract you while he sneaks up a gun with the other hand to blow your brains out. She doesn't do that. Instead, she says, "I'm pulling the plug on this one. There's always next year." Which is pretty much the same thing.

I turn around and tell her to get lost—give or take an expletive or two.

She tries to tell me that I can go to the park tomorrow or the next day and run laps there to finish the distance. And she, liberal, magnanimous soul that she is, will still count it as a marathon finish. But she doesn't want me out on the course anymore. Then she reminds me again that there's always next year.

My first and most immediate thought is how the hell did someone like her ever get involved with Achilles? The whole point is that I am running the New York City Marathon, and that means following the blue line wherever it takes me. For as long as it takes me. If it were just about running the 26.2 miles, I could run the circumference of the park four times, on any given day of the week, and call it a marathon. Or anything else I have a mind to call it.

As for there always being next year, if there is one thing that MS has taught me, it's that when you come right down to it, there is only right now. I have learned over the years to use the words *always* and *never* quite sparingly and to use the word *now* as frequently as possible.

For me, it is right here, right now. I'm not getting into the car. I'm not quitting the race. I tell her to stop patronizing me and to get her hands off me. Friends can touch me. She is obviously not a friend. I ask her to give me one good reason why we should be disqualified so far into the race, so close to the finish line. She responds with what she considers not one but two good reasons. First, because she has decided to set a time limit for Achilles members, and we have passed it. And second, because she says so. She points out that she is the head coach for Achilles and has every right to make such judgment calls as she sees fit. For the good of the club and for the good of the individual. Whether we see it that way or not, and whether we like it or not is totally irrelevant.

The anger I have been barely holding in check finally blows up in her face. "You knew how long it was going to take me from the very beginning! Based on my half marathon, I never could have finished in less than eighteen hours. If you never had any intention of letting me finish, then why did you let me even start? What the hell do you think we're doing out here, playing a game? Now you're tired of playing, so it's time for us to go home. No one is requiring anything of you. You don't have to follow us.

You don't have to be at the finish line! Is there any physical reason why I should stop? No. OK, so I limp more than I did at the beginning of the day, but hell, I limp more at the end of EVERY day than I do at the start. So what? Am I coherent? Yes. Do I know exactly what I'm doing? Yes. SO, WHAT IS YOUR DAMNED PROBLEM? You tell me there's always next year. Well, maybe there is and maybe there isn't. But from where I'm standing, all I can see and all I can know is *right now*. And from moment to moment, all I can do is go with what I've got."

I look around to my friends for their reaction. They are nodding in emphatic agreement. Marsha, bless her heart, has been pushed way past her level of tolerance. She's been there from the very beginning. From way before even that first night at Achilles. We've been friends for a long time. She tells this official to get back in her car and go the home. If you're not for us, she points out, then you're against us. And if you're against us, then get the off the course. Get the hell out of our way and let us finish what we started.

The woman opens her mouth to reply, thinks better of it, and gets back in the car. With gears grinding and doors slamming, she takes off into the night.

For the next half-hour, as we keep running through the long dark night, I am furious. I am devastated. I feel betrayed. Tricked. Jerked around. But I am also scared, because I don't know if I have pissed off my entire track club to the point where I'll never again be allowed to run. There is the distinct possibility that I may end up as a disqualified nonfinisher for ignoring the direct instructions of a race official.

It's a far more complicated situation than just two different personalities at odds here. There are larger issues of common sense and personal responsibility involved. Where in this society do you stop capitulating to someone else's definition of good sense? When do you stop accepting abuse being perpetrated on you "for your own good"? When do you embrace the risk, take the plunge and reclaim a small piece of the universe for your very own, if only for one night?

It is not till a couple of days after the marathon, at the Achilles pizza party, that I find out what the real bottom line is. She who was all sound and fury had absolutely no authority whatsoever. She wasn't acting under the auspices of Achilles, and she certainly wasn't handling anyone's agenda but her own. If I had obeyed her instructions and quit, it would have been for nothing. Absolutely nothing at all.

When I run into her at the gathering, she greets me with a venomous smile. In lieu of the simple word "Congratulations," which would have done nicely in the situation, she turns on her heel and hurls a parting shot: "If you've achieved nothing else, you've at least lost some much-needed weight." The following year, we bring a bunch of really tacky plastic flowers along with us. When we get to those same steps, we set up a memorial shrine to the woman who tried to make us go home.

Finally, that first year, we get to the park. We are exhausted but exhilarated. We hang out under the street lamps in a tight little cluster, poring over our now tattered copy of the marathon map, because we have no idea of where we are or what's up. We don't even know for sure where the finish line is. There is no banner, no clock ticking off the seconds and minutes and hours.

For a few minutes, we don't even know for sure

whether we're on the course. After twenty thousand runners, the blue line gets a little faded, and then just after you enter the park it disappears altogether. It is right at the twenty-six mile mark, just 285 yards from the end, where the course cuts off the road, across a patch of grass, and onto the final finishing stretch.

Finish-line problems notwithstanding, at least three of our crew have an even more pressing problem at the moment. We really have to go to the bathroom. Over the last few hours, the lack of public facilities has turned into a major drama. How do you do what you've got to do when there's no place to do it? Hester, Marsha, and I head for the bushes. Justin goes off in search of a tree.

Since it's almost two o'clock in the morning, it never dawns on us that anyone could possibly be in the park. Modesty is no longer a major issue. We're just too tired and too desperate to care. Inadvertently, we "moon" a passing biker. He almost runs into a tree. We are literally doubled over with laughter. We sincerely hope it "was good for him," because it was really great for us.

With empty bladders and happy hearts, we finally figure out where we are: we have passed the 26-mile mark. We stop to hug and congratulate one another. We have survived. We have endured. And now it is not just my marathon, but their marathon as well. They have been with me all through the night, and all of our personal journeys have become knotted together.

It is three minutes before two in the morning when we finally get to the finish line painted on the pavement. We don't really see it, because it's now the dead of night. Mental note for next year: bring flashlights.

I do what I will always do when I cross the line. I throw

up my right arm and let out a war whoop that must have woken up half the West Side. Hester is at my side, as she has been every step of the way. Then and forever. We had started out on a great bridge in far-away Staten Island that morning as friendly strangers—acquaintances with a common goal. And now, nineteen hours and fifty-seven minutes of our lives later, we are friends for life. I didn't know it, but Hester had confided a wish to her journal that year, that she have a special friend to run the marathon with. And her wish has come true—for both of us.

Although we've crossed the finish line, our journey isn't quite over. Before the race began, we were given a phone number that we're supposed to call when we finish so that our time will be official. Now I am in the park in the middle of the night, looking for a pay phone, so that I can call the "results person"—just a regular person who has agreed to take down the finishing times for late Achilles runners. I find the phone and a coin, get the number, and make the call.

I have just done what I think is the greatest thing in my life, and I want it to be properly recorded. It is after two A.M. and the "results person" is sound asleep. When I call him to say that I have just finished the marathon, the most wonderful accomplishment of my life, I obviously wake him up out a dead sleep. He says, "Get a freakin' life," and hangs up the phone.

None of it has turned out the way anyone could have guessed or predicted, except that we have reached and crossed the finish line. That much I always knew. But it wasn't like anything I had imagined. It never occurred to me that we would finish in the pitch dark, searching for the actual finish line. Or that we would have any of the adventures that we did, with Meena and her mom and all the people we met along the way. I never imagined that I would pee in the bushes, moon a biker, or come to blows with a disgruntled track club official. As my late great-Grandma Celia would say, "So who knew already?"

I learn a lot about myself and about others that first year. It's a good foundation for future lessons. I realize that other people's sense of commitment is far different from mine. I stop making them wrong and obsessing about their omissions. I learn the difference between accountability and blame.

I also now know that there are people who are willing to end my run simply because it is inconvenient for them or because I don't fit their picture of what a "real runner" should look like. And I have gained new insight into the nature of instruction sheets and "results people." They have absolutely nothing to do with reality if you finish at two o'clock in the morning.

That first year, I also learn what is perhaps one of the most important and enduring lessons of my life: the strength and power of friendship. In the years to come, I will learn that lesson again and again. My friends will teach me. I am deeply grateful to all those who have made the journey with Hester and me, whether it was for two miles or the entire marathon. Each and every one of my friends has brought unique gifts and talents to the journey. It has been their love and laughter that buoyed my spirits and kept me in motion long after the body began to shut down. They have taught me all that I know of "the winning spirit." And they have taught me well.

Finally, I learn that first year what the marathon really is. Perhaps what it was always meant to be. I know now that

I do not need spectators. I do not need medals. The day has been a gift. The perfect gift. My heart is full, and it is more than enough. Perhaps it is more than most people could hope for in a lifetime. It is an eternity of emotion compressed into a single moment in time.

CHAPTER 4

WHEN I PUT on my running number, it is like putting on a super cape, a shield. It is my magic amulet that for one day lets me go anywhere in the city that the blue line of the marathon goes.

I'm not näive. I live in the East Village in New York City, and if I didn't have some street smarts, I couldn't survive there. It's just that I see my number as the passport that enables me to cross borders into places I have never visited. My first race confirmed that belief. The number announced my status as a marathoner, and people opened their doors and their hearts to me—in as many different ways as there are people in this city.

For instance, when we get into Upper Manhattan and the Bronx, we meet different sorts of spectator. We notice kids, a half dozen or more, hanging out on the street corners around the projects, long after they should have been in bed if they had any notion of attending school the following morning. Gang members protecting their turf. And here comes this gaggle of women and a guy in a wheelchair.

That first year I walked right up to them and said, "Hi," pointed to the race number. "Yup," I went on, "still out here doin' the marathon. Only six point two miles to go."

So immediately, they got who I was and what I was about. They didn't have time to react or to do anything, because, by walking up to them, I'd caught them completely off guard. The thought that this white woman who looks like a giant Muppet, or maybe a Raggedy Ann doll, with big eyes, huge rhinestone earrings, a turtle cape, and the whole get-up, would walk right up and say, "Hi," totally disarmed them.

There was one group on the Willis Avenue Bridge, going into the Bronx, who wanted to know just who in creation was this woman and what the hell was she up to on their bridge? By walking up and telling them, I answered the question and stated my mission. They could deal with it then. It was cool.

Invariably, they join the adventure. "Yo, home girl! You can still be a winner no matter how long it takes."

So I adopt an expresion of mock horror and stop dead in my tracks. "Wait a minute," I say. "Lemme get this straight. I can *still* be a winner? What's with the word *still*? Does that mean that someone else has already crossed the finish line? I mean, it's only midnight. The night is still young."

They're totally on my side now, and they crack up laughing. I join their laughter. "Yeah," I say, "you just go ahead and laugh. I was counting on winning the Mercedes and driving it home. And if the car wasn't ready, I could use the $35,000 winner's check for cab fare. What do you think? Should I finish anyway, just for the hell of it?"

Amid peals of laughter, there is a resounding "Yes!" The sound of that word and all it implies will echo in my heart for many miles to come. The first block of those miles we are accompanied by the kids. We have an escort.

One of the group starts to circle me, inspecting my shawl. "Teenage Mutant Ninja Turtle," he finally decides.

"No," I correct him. "It's Flash the Miracle Racing Turtle"

"Are the earrings real?" he asks, pointing to the gaudy baubles I wear. "As real as you can get for $7.50," I deadpan.

At the end of the block that marks the border of their territory is another gang of kids, hanging out on another corner. My gang introduces us to the new gang as "the crazy people still out here doin' this thing." With that, they hand us off as neatly as a football. And so we go through the Bronx, one gang handing us off to the next, escorting us on our way, becoming part of the adventure.

A year later, when I return for my second marathon, the same kids are waiting for us, and more have joined them. One of the local TV stations did a story on me right before the marathon, so I have some added cachet.

A kid who saw the story says, "You know, I wondered if you were a real person or just someone they made up to hype the race. Guess you're real enough if you're still out here doing this thing. I look at you and think of all the things I don't think I can do. You make me wonder if I shouldn't think again."

"Hey," I say, touched by his words. "Thanks for letting me know that our being out here means something to you. You're right. You should think again. If you can dream it and you can plan it, you can do it. I really believe that."

Yes, the number is magic again, so we continue our journey, moment to moment, block to block. The youth of the Bronx, in their inimitable way, ensure our safe passage through what many people think of as one of the most dangerous neighborhoods on the marathon route. We wonder whether on any other day or under any other set of circumstances our rapport would be the same. It is impossible to know, and perhaps it's better not to think about it at all. Some questions are best left unanswered.

On my second marathon, before we even get to the gangs, we meet a different and deadly menace. It's around Mile 20, just past the Willis Avenue Bridge. There are five of us this year; along the route we have picked up various friends who will do portions of the race but not the entire course.

It's deserted up here in the Bronx. But maybe that's just normal for Sunday night. We pass a man bent over his car engine, wrench in hand. I wonder why he's out here so late by himself. I guess he wonders the same thing about us. As we pass, he stares at us and lifts his wrench to shoulder level. I cannot tell if it's a greeting or a warning.

Marsha and I lag twenty or thirty feet behind Hester and the rest of our friends. A serious mistake. We should be sticking together from here to the finish line for safety's sake. But before we can catch up, two men spot us from across the street and make a beeline for us. Marsha turns to me and says, "Oh, God, Zoe. This is it." There isn't time or breath to say anything more as they bear down on us.

The one in the lead has his hand in the pocket of his windbreaker, and I can see the distinct, unmistakable outline of a gun. As he comes closer, he pulls his hand partly out and lets us see the butt, just to confirm and magnify our fears. We are easy pickings. Four women and a man in a wheelchair. A low-impact terrorist warm-up for a big night uptown.

My number is supposed to grant me an exemption; it never occurred to me that something like this could happen. I lock eyes with him for a moment. He sees our marathon numbers. His eyes turn into question marks. I'll never know whether I actually said this or just thought it at the top of my lungs: "Whatever it is, don't even think it!"

Just a few feet away, he keeps checking us out. Runners? Could this be right? He makes a noise under his breath, something like, "Oh, Christ," and holds his free arm out to stop his friend from doing whatever he had planned. Then he signals his partner to back off. It is simultaneously a gesture of salvation and of dismissal. Whatever his original intentions, for reasons best known only to himself, we are spared.

He passes us without saying a word, but there is a barely perceptible shake of his head, left to right, and again that hand gesture of dismissal. It is impossible to read what he is thinking or feeling. Incredulity? Annoyance? Boredom? He walks out of our lives and into the darkness, perhaps in search of more lucrative prey.

I suppress an overwhelming urge to run after him. Part of me wants to beat him into the ground for frightening us so badly. Who the hell does he think he is? What gives him the right to decide whether we live or die? The other part of me wants to shake his hand and say, "Thank you." Thank you for not holding us up, shooting us, or killing us. Thank you for sparing our lives. I am trapped between rage and gratitude. Not a very good place to be.

Before we have a chance to recover, we are into the projects, saying hello to the gangs. They remember us and pass us through again. We get through the Bronx with no further problems, cross the Madison Avenue Bridge, and, alone again, enter Harlem.

As we pass Mile 21, something is wrong. Deadly wrong.

I feel it in every fiber of my being. This must be how it feels to be inside a tornado, locked in that momentary air-less, lifeless vacuum that precedes the whirlwind. The pro-verbial calm before the storm. My mortality is a visceral creature with a life of its own. It lopes alongside of me dressed in yellow and red. The colors of bile and blood. There is not enough air to breathe, and you know the ante has just gone up. Big time.

I have fleeting but intense thoughts of the Central Park jogger, that anonymous female runner who barely survived a brutal gang rape while out training for the marathon. Was there a moment, one solitary moment, distinct from all the rest, when she knew for sure that she was looking at the end of her life? For me, this is that moment.

I look at my friends, and my worst fears are mirrored in their eyes. The light-hearted banter that has accented so much of our day lapses into an ominous silence. Instinc-tively, we close ranks. I think of wagon trains and caravans readying themselves for an onslaught of unknown dimen-sions.

Although it is the middle of the night, there are many people in the streets, so many that at first I think we have stumbled on some bizarre block party. But it's more like a flea market, sans the tables and endless array of merchan-dise. Apparently, we have walked into what must be New York's largest open-air drug mart. You can't live where I do and not pass the small-time dealers saying, "Check it out" from the sides of their mouths. But these people are brazenly standing in the street, selling stuff. A whole other story.

They stand in groups of three and four, at least two

groups on each side of the street per block. They are dressed in jeans and jackets or sweatshirts. Low-level guys. Each group has a dealer and at least two cohorts.

They spot us immediately and begin signaling to one another. Shrill whistles pass from one side of the street to the other. Monosyllabic shouts punctuate the night air, heralding our passage.

We are civilians trapped in a war zone, aliens in a foreign country. No passports. Ignorant of the language and customs. Even my magic running number is no longer a valid ID. With every passing moment, we move deeper into the dealing, and our chances of safe extradition grow dimmer and fewer. I'm wondering whether they are going to let us live, but there's nowhere to run, nowhere to hide. We have no choice but to continue.

We do so in silence. It's one thing to walk up to the kids in the Bronx gangs and try to make contact with them, possibly even befriend them. But these people on the street tonight are not the kind of people you walk up to and say, "Guess what? I'm still running the marathon." Not if you want to continue living.

The vibes are horrifying. People are reaching into their pockets, the body language of the street that says, "I'm armed. I'm dangerous." I have no idea how many blocks we cover. It seems like forever. And all the while, the whistles and shouts direct every eye on us.

Fear gives birth to absurdity, and for one ridiculous moment I almost expect Rod Serling to materialize from the shadows and give his two-minute soliloquy introducing us as the stars of tonight's episode of *The Twilight Zone*. "The last runners in the New York City Marathon . . . Crossing the twenty-one mile mark . . . Suddenly displaced from time and circumstance . . . Are now entering . . . the Twilight Zone."

I have never thought of myself as näive. I moved to the infamous Alphabet City in the East Village twenty years ago, long before it was fashionable to live there. I've gone to my share of tenants' meetings and fought as hard as I know how to keep my building safe from the perils of both drugs and gentrification. I've kicked crack dealers out of my hallway and refused entrance to people I know have come to buy drugs. I've survived a holdup and an attempted rape. All things considered, I've paid my dues. In my own terms, I'm a hard-core New Yorker. But nothing—nothing—in the context of my life experience could have prepared me for what we're up against tonight. We are in the greatest city in the world, but it looks and feels more like Beirut. The apartments and row houses that line the streets at one time were fine buildings. Now they loom over us like stripped and scuttled battleships. The windows, many of them broken, are like so many empty sockets, staring down on us. Here and there a bare lightbulb or candle burns behind a grime-coated pane. We feel no comfort in the glow, only terror.

In the midst of this, a black and expensive foreign sports car pulls up to one of the groups. We see a package and an envelope change hands. We have no idea what they are, but we know we're not supposed to see. The plot thickens.

Someone in our group starts reading the license plate on the car. Out loud. It is one of those stupid things you do sometimes, when your thoughts take voice, seemingly on their own. Here, it's a potentially fatal faux pas in a place where forgiveness is bought with blood.

A few years in the future, the dealers would be grabbing

for their cellular phones to spread the word. But this is 1989, and cellular phones are not yet the rage. Instead, the word passes with a newly urgent flurry of whistles and calls. Deafening to our ragged senses, they zig-zag back and forth across and down the street.

Then, from out of nowhere, a beat-up old car materializes at a phone booth, and a man gets out to make a call. We reach him in mid-dial. When he sees us, he runs his hands across his eyes, as if we are a hallucination, as if maybe we'll vanish when he opens his eyes again. No such luck. We're still there.

He is a heavyset black man, maybe forty years old. Whoever he is, for him to be up there, willing to get out of his car and leave it unattended, with the keys in it, to make a phone call means that he has the respect of the neighborhood. He has to be a heavy-duty player in one way or another. We are afraid to talk, nearly afraid to breathe. He initiates the conversation. "Good God," he gasps, "what the hell are you folks doing up here at this hour?"

We don't have time to answer. The numbers on our chests have registered. "Ah, the last runners. Of course. Who else could you be? Ran the marathon myself ten years ago. Well, if you've made it this far, I guess you've got to finish what you started. Just answer me this one question before you go. You know you're in trouble, right? We're talking serious trouble here."

Yeah, we tell him, although *trouble* isn't quite the word we think describes what we are in. We ask if he's got any suggestions for us. He runs his hands over his eyes again. Damn. We still don't disappear. "Yeah," he says, and he actually laughs, the last sound we expect to hear. "I got a suggestion for you. I suggest that you should have finished about eight hours ago and should never have been up here at this hour to start out with. But seein' as you're up here now, lemme see what I can do."

He tells us there's an all-night fast-food restaurant a couple of blocks ahead. He'll let the people there know we're on our way, and they'll let us come inside to use the bathroom and get ourselves back together again. "Meanwhile," he says, "lemme see what I can do. Lemme talk to some people in the street. Know what I mean? All I ask is that when you leave the restaurant, get the hell out of here just as fast as you can. Don't look left. Don't look right. Don't look back. Just get the hell out. If you can make it to the Park entrance at 102nd Street, you should be OK. But till then, no guarantees. Understand? No guarantees. Good luck to you."

He gives us a thumbs-up and walks off to the nearest group. We hear snatches of conversation as we move on. One phrase in particular leaps out. It quickens the pulse and chills the blood. "Just let them go. They're not worth it."

This is the bottom line to explain why we're still alive. We're not worth it.

In the next couple of blocks, my life flashes before my eyes at least a dozen times. This short distance seems to take longer than the whole damned marathon. At last, we arrive at the restaurant. The fast-food sandwich place is more like a fortress than a restaurant. Thick, bulletproof glass extends from the ceiling to the counter. The food is delivered through a double window controlled from inside so that one plate of glass is always between server and customer. As far as we're concerned, it's Nirvana.

True to his word, our protector has made arrangements for us. We can come in and pull ourselves together. They will allow us to use the bathroom on the safe side of the glass, a courtesy not extended to the usual clientele. But Justin cannot come in, his wheelchair will not fit through the door. We take turns going inside, one of us always staying with Justin.

As I make my way to the bathroom, I am shaking. A million conflicting thoughts flash through my head. Every crime-related newspaper headline and TV newscast I have ever seen plays through my head. Simultaneously. In 3-D and Dolby Surround Sound.

The only thing I have ever been afraid of is not having enough to finish. It never dawned on me that someone might take a sawed-off shotgun and blow my head off. Where do you take a stand in this life? What distinguishes a positive, life-affirming choice from a willful act of self-destruction? I honestly don't know, and it's not likely I'm going to figure it out within the next few minutes.

As I reach the bathroom, I am hit by an emotional jolt that leaves me weak and in a cold sweat. For me, this is the Twilight Zone, but for hundreds and perhaps even thousands of people, this is home. This is their neighborhood. I have a choice as to whether I want to be here or not. At any given moment, I can walk away and never look back. For me, it's that simple. But what about the children who grow up here? What I hold as an unforgettable, once-in-a-lifetime experience is, for them, everyday life. The thought of kids living with this as their everyday lives is abhorrent to me. This kind of horror shouldn't be what controls peoples' lives.

I close the bathroom door and throw up.

Afterward, I am not at peace. Not by any means. I am both enraged and frightened. From moment to moment one gains dominance over the other. Although I would be fine about hailing a cab and getting my friends the hell out of there, I will not get off this course. Not for anyone. Guns or no guns. Drugs or no drugs.

I know there are no easy or magical solutions for drugs or homelessness. What it would take on a legislative, fiscal, or military level to cure what ails us, I couldn't begin to guess. I don't even want to. But I understand what it would take on an emotional and spiritual level. It would take this city rising up as a whole, one awesome organism transcending the artificial boundaries of race, class, and neighborhood. A benevolent beast rising from the depths of our collective being in such a state of rage and effrontery that, inch by inch and block by block, it would reclaim our streets, our parks, our homes. And most of all, our pride.

How many more blocks, how many more miles, and how many more neighborhoods will we quietly surrender in the name of common sense and self-preservation? How many more activities will I eliminate from my life simply because they are not safe to do anymore?

This is my city. I want it back. I have a right to be here. I have a right to run this marathon, whether it's one P.M., one A.M., or any time in between. I will not go away. I cannot and will not quit. I will not alter my course. If I give up tonight, then I will have lost something very special. The New York City Marathon and everything it stands for in my life will become just another crime statistic. It will die a lonely, ignominious death, without so much as the requiem of a police report to mark its demise.

Later, when it has all had a chance to gel, I realize that this is the same reason I have never moved from where I live, even during harder times, when it started going downhill with the advent of bodegas that sold crack. You can move out, but that's the same as throwing up your hands and saying, "You win." That's why, when a crack dealer moved into our building, all the decent residents banded together and went to his place, knocked on the door, and demanded that it stop. Because there is no such thing as a little cancer. No such thing as an acceptable level of evil. And you know what? It stopped.

This is the commitment we make in that restaurant. I ask my friends to rethink their dedication to staying on the course. These last hours have made demands on them both physically and emotionally that far exceed the boundaries of friendship, loyalty, and commitment. They shouldn't have to risk their lives to run a marathon in this or any other city. They are here because of me. This isn't part of what they signed up for.

I feel responsible for their safety and will support any or all of them in dropping out. I will figure out a way to get them home. I remember what the man said. No guarantees between here and 102nd Street.

They know, and they have reached the same conclusion I have. They are tired and drained but determined. Hester throws her arm around my shoulders and says, "Hey, home girl! Yeah, you! You better jet-propel those sneakers of yours. I think it's time for the miracle mile."

It is the perfect note to sound. Everyone laughs. We take one final look across the street. Our guardian angel is still out there "talkin' to some people," repeating that thing about our not being worth it. We'd like to say thank you. We'd like to say good-bye. Who is this guy anyway? A drug dealer? An undercover cop? A neighborhood resident who's put his life on the line for us? He's saved our lives, and we don't know a thing about him, not even his name. We'd like to say a million and one things, but we know we'd better take the man's advice and get the hell out of here.

We hit the road, the drug dealers behind us, we know not what ahead. Ten blocks down the course, we see a police car. We flag it down, figuring maybe we'll get a police escort to the park. The cruiser flashes its lights in response to our waves and pulls over to the curb. We scramble toward it, but just then the light turns from red to green, and it drives away. The officers inside saw us. We know they did. Somehow we're not surprised at their reaction. It doesn't matter. With or without them, we are going to finish this race. Wait up for me, New York City; your last runner is in the final stretch of her long journey home.

Finally, we arrive at the relative safety of Central Park. It is still more than two miles to the finish, but we feel as if we are in the Promised Land. Our adrenaline is depleted, but our spirits are high. We divvy up the remaining food and water and are on our way to another finish line. Alone in the dark. My time will be 20:57, one hour longer than my first marathon.

THAT SUMMER, A movement begins within Road Runners to take the slowest runners off the course at some point on First Avenue and run them straight across to the park instead of having them go up to the Bronx and down through Harlem. In Central Park, we would run a couple of loops—as if that's a safe proposition—to get in the required miles to make up a marathon. They call it an "alternate route."

There are a lot of valid reasons to do that. God forbid

anything ever happens to a runner out finishing long after the main body. Who would be responsible? Sure, you sign a waiver before you begin the race, but lawyers do what lawyers do. Other runners than myself are involved. There is legitimate reason to worry.

Some people think I'm being selfish by fighting the proposal, that I'm not being a team player. They are afraid that I could jeopardze the right of all disabled athletes to run. For me, there are larger issues involved. I feel this is a glaring illustration of why the city is in the mess it's in. In essence, what they are asking me to do is no different from throwing up my hands in resignation and moving out of my neighborhood. To accept the fact that we can not reclaim this city, if only for one night, is unthinkable.

When I'm out on the marathon course following that blue line, I get to go where the best of them and the rest of them have been before me. I go where the big kids have gone that day. More than twenty thousand other people just like me, with all their hopes, dreams, and self-doubts, run that same course and cross that same finish line. This matters to me a great deal. If this were about mileage, I could run around my living room fifty thousand times and call it a marathon. But so what? Who cares? You can't tell me it's the same thing.

I have always believed that people in this country who are disabled, or different in some way, are forced to run enough alternate courses in their lives, and I'll be damned if I'll allow the marathon to become one more alternate course. Hester and I discuss this at great length and decide to limit the number of friends who go with us beyond 100th Street, where the neighborhoods begin to get more dangerous. We don't want people putting themselves at risk. For ourselves, we believe we cannot back down.

Even before the alternate course was suggested, we knew we needed help. That spring, I post notices in some of the police precincts to see whether we can get some off-duty cops to tag along for a few critical miles. I don't really expect any takers, and I am right. I wrack my brain about where to go next, and then it pops into my head. The Guardian Angels.

CHAPTER 5

THE GUARDIAN ANGELS were born in New York City, on February 13, 1979, the child of Curtis Sliwa. Curtis was born and raised in Brooklyn, New York, the son of a blue-collar, working-class family. He worked as a night manager for McDonald's and his constant exposure to crime in the streets and the subways motivated him to start the volunteer citizen, anticrime group now known as the Guardian Angels. His idea was to give young men and women in poor neighborhoods an alternative to street gangs. Instead of committing crimes, these kids would fight them. He dressed them in T-shirts with the Guardian Angel logo and trademark red berets. They were trained in the martial arts as well as in CPR and first-aid skills. Initially, they created enormous controversy because people saw them as vigilantes.

But the Angels have lived up to their name. They patrol subway lines plagued by crime, escort women home from subway and bus stops in neighborhoods where serial rapists are at work, and frequently act as negotiators between warring ethnic groups in some of the more volatile sections of the city. Eventually controversy takes a back seat to meritorious achievement and the Angels give a new twist to the old axiom "Actions speak louder than words."

By 1997 they are a worldwide organization, with thirty

chapters reaching from New York City to Japan and Australia. They incorporate the best of those early years with a brand-new sense of global empowerment that will propel them well into the twenty-first century.

Their fourteen-week afterschool club is geared toward developing leadership skills in high school students. Each weekly segment deals with a crucial topic, such as personal responsibility and community volunteerism. The graduation ceremony, held on a weekend, is a backpacking and camping expedition arranged through Outward Bound.

Graffiti paint-outs are organized to bring divergent community members together to work on common basic goals, thereby setting the foundation for larger cooperative ventures in the future. Start small. Think big.

In the parks, they work side by side with the police department on in-line skating and bike patrols. They serve as a visual deterrent to crime and promote a general atmosphere of safety and harmony. Time and necessity have transformed what was once an adversarial relationship between the police and the Angels into a mutually beneficial partnership.

The ominous issues of drug abuse and gang warfare are addressed head on by the members of their speakers' bureaus. Angels go into schools and not only "tell it like it is" but also give kids a vision of the future. A vision of how it might be to live in a world where they are no longer controlled by circumstances or environment. A world where they can take these factors, turn them around, and use them as tools for making a difference not only in their own "hood," but ultimately in the world.

It has become apparent, to even the most casual of observers or the staunchest of critics, that the Guardian Angels have evolved into an organization that New Yorkers can really be proud of.

Back in 1991, when I call them before my third marathon, all I really know about them is that they are probably my best hope for thumbing my nose at the "alternate route" ruling and making it to the finish line in one piece.

When I make that first phone call, I am put through directly to Curtis Sliwa. He is courteous, attentive, and concerned. After I explain my problem, he asks me to submit a written request to the Angels, which will be submitted to their review board. I do so, and they get back to me almost immediately, agreeing to take us on for my third marathon. It is the beginning of what will be a lifelong friendship between me, my marathon team, and the Guardian Angels.

We don't really need the Angels for the whole route, just from upper Manhattan on to the finish line—the last nine or ten miles. That first year a friend suggests the Cafe 79 as a good place for us to hook up. It is a family-style restaurant, right along the marathon route, and is the perfect place to take our one legitimate meal break for the day to fortify ourselves for the tough miles and long hours ahead.

We get to the Cafe 79, sit down, and wait for the Angels to arrive. No one knows exactly what to expect. When they arrive, we see these four incredibly young kids, and they see this woman who is, by their standards, old enough to be their grandmother. They take it all in: the rhinestone earrings, the Flash the Miracle Racing Turtle shawl, my trademark iridescent purple eye makeup. Their reaction is absolutely priceless. They look at me as if I've just stepped out of *The Rocky Horror Picture Show*. They seem unsure if they are meant to protect me from New York, or vice versa. I look at Hester, she looks at me, and it's everything we can do to keep from cracking up.

The meal quickly turns into a "so how young are they?" joke. The punchline? They are so young that they have to call their mothers to let them know where they are and what time they'll be home. Neither Curtis nor they had any idea that it would involve being out all night. But any doubts we have about their youthful appearance vanish the instant we hit the streets. They are in contact with head-quarters via mobile radio units every two or three blocks. Their entire attitude is as serious and professional as that of an elite army patrol on a top-priority mission.

The first test of our cohesiveness as a team occurs before we even cross into the Bronx. A bunch of kids from the projects come out on bikes and start circling us, trying to disorient us. The old hit-and-run gambit. Confuse us, make off with whatever is easily snatchable, and take off at light-ning speed. The Angels are having none of this. We keep our cool and they walk us through it. After six or seven blocks, the kids are out of their turf and have grown tired of the chase. They disappear into the night.

Eventually, Curtis sends out some older Angels for the late shift. But these young Angels have shown me that per-formance is not necessarily connected to age. They know the code of the streets. We were as safe with them as we would have been in an armored truck. I will never again make an arbitrary, age-biased judgment that anyone is either too young or too old to do his or her job well, no matter what that job may be.

For the first couple of years, Curtis assigns us two teams, one to relieve the other. But invariably, the first team always stays with us to the end, because they want what there is to be had. The finish line. Instead of chasing drug dealers from block to block, here is something visceral. Something they can hold as their outcome for the night. Something with a happy ending. One year, in the middle of the night, one of them came up to me and said, "You know, this is not just your race. This is about my life." He got it. Totally.

Over the years, I've come to understand that different people "get it" in completely different ways. Whenever I need a reason to smile or a moment to hold on to when the going gets rough, I remember an Angel named Cyclops and what has come to be known as "The Legend of the Purple Gloves."

Weatherwise, 1995 is beyond a doubt the worst of all my marathons. We begin the race in howling winds, bitter cold rain, and snow showers on the Verrazano Bridge. We are chilled and soaked to the bone, which sets a precedent for the rest of the day. During the night, with the wind-chill factor, the temperature drops down into the teens. Wind gusts howl at more than forty-five miles per hour. Not all the Angels are prepared for such inclement weather.

Luckily, I have brought along an extra pair of gloves, which I offer to Cyclops. He's now faced with a dilemma. Warm hands or bright purple gloves. What's a guy to do? Normally, his wearing such gloves would give his comrades license to tease him unmercifully, to the point where he'd have to take them off. Knowing that, I announce that no one is allowed to tease him about the purple gloves. We're not talking about a fashion statement here; we're talking about frostbite.

Throughout the night Cyclops shares the gloves with the rest of the Angels: one hand in a pocket, the other encased in a purple glove. The warmth they generate is not just a matter of fiber and fabric. The gloves take on an energy and a life of their own. They are about friendship. They are about endurance. They are about winning. They cross the line with us the following morning.

When the race is over, I tell Cyclops it would give me great pleasure if he would keep the gloves as a souvenir of our time together, as a reminder of the finish line. Cyclops goes home and shows the gloves to his mother. She stores them in a special box and puts them away, a family treasure that is taken out from time to time and shown to friends and relatives. They will never be worn again.

Never think what the Guardian Angels do is that easy. Whenever they sign on for my marathon, they don't know what that commitment might mean or require of them in the course of the night. For all intents and purposes, it is an act of blind faith. But when you sign on for something, you take what comes with it—good, bad, or indifferent. The Angels are with us to escort and protect us. That is their promise. And the power of that promise is the cornerstone of my unshakable belief that, at any given moment, they would lay down their lives to make good on that promise. I know this as truth, because once they almost did.

We are in that horrible netherworld where the gargoyles come out in the middle of the night and you never know what might appear around the next corner or down the next block. This is where the drug supermarket was. Here, bare light bulbs and flickering candles cast garish, writhing shadows in the blasted-out buildings inhabited by crackheads and hookers. Emaciated women, thin as rails, wearing almost nothing in the long, cold night, try to get enough money to feed both their kids and their habits.

We are making our way slowly and painfully through this urban hell, when a black car with black windows rolls slowly past us. Its boom box is going at a million decibels, so loud the ground shakes beneath us. The Angels' antennae are up immediately. They're wired and ready to move. But the car pulls away, turns, and disappears.

A few minutes later, the same pounding beat thunders behind us once again. The car is back. The Angels get on their walkie-talkies and alert their headquarters that we're being set up for a drive-by shooting. We are in the middle of one of the worst blocks on the whole marathon course, alongside what the Angels call the Crack Hilton, a row of burned-out drug dens.

With a lump in my throat and a knot in my stomach, I look up at Dragon, the Angel closest to me, and ask, "So what do we do now. What's the game plan here?"

"If that car window opens even so much as a crack," he explains, "I'm going to throw you on the ground and throw myself on top of you. We'll try to roll out of their line of fire. Let's just hope that the crazies in the Crack Hilton don't think it's a shoot-out between them and the jerks in the car. If they do, we could get caught in the crossfire. And that'll be a problem. A real problem. And then . . . And then, we pray for the best. That's all we can do. Pray for the best. In the meantime, just act natural.

Don't turn around. Don't talk to your friends. The other Angels will look after them just as I'll look after you. Ignore the car. Ignore the noise. Just keep walking. If the situation changes, believe me, you'll be the first to know."

"But why us?" I persist.

He shrugs his shoulders. "Hard to believe, but it's probably nothing personal. To get into some gangs, you have to kill a total stranger. And at three in the morning," he quips, trying to make light of it, "there's not much out here that's stranger than us."

It could all be as terrifyingly simple as that. An initiation ritual.

Over the din of the boom box, we can hear voices raised in argument inside the car. A decision is being reached. Perhaps they also are wary of engaging the occupants of the Crack Hilton in an accidental shoot-out. Nothing will mess up the shine on a brand-new car faster than a couple of dozen rounds of well-placed ammo from a semiautomatic weapon.

Or maybe they have realized that we definitely don't fit the normal profile of those who are out in their neighborhood in the middle of the night. Kill a hooker, execute a junkie: easy prey. The city would probably chalk it up to another unfortunate life-come-to-a-sad-but-predictable end. Kill a gaggle of runners and some Guardian Angels; that's another story. A high-profile, high-status kill, for sure. But not one without dire consequences. Pursuit, capture, and relentless prosecution would all be inevitable.

For whatever reason, the car window does not open. They stalk us for another block and then, with tires screeching and boom box still blaring, drive away. We finish that year's marathon without further incident.

In 1993, much to our dismay, we find out that human predators are not the only source of potential danger along the marathon route.

We have stopped for a break at Eighty-ninth Street and Fifth Avenue. I am near my limit of endurance. Perhaps I have even surpassed it and am just too tired, too stubborn, or too dumb to know the difference. My left leg keeps going spastic on me, at times refusing to move and at other times shaking uncontrollably. Hester feeds me two Advils, and as I wait for them to kick in, I sprawl on a park bench, eyes closed, disconnecting and reconnecting the wires, re-routing the garbled neurological signals so that we can finish the last few miles.

From somewhere on the periphery of my consciousness, I hear a noise. Where have I heard it before? It's a low-pitched squeal accompanied by a rustling in the bushes behind us on the Fifth Avenue side of our route. Squirrels, I decide; park's full of them.

Still sitting there, I can't get out of my head the idea that I've heard this sound and that it wasn't from a squirrel. It's a humming kind of squeal, and it's getting more and more intense. Where have I heard this before?

And then, with a start, my eyes fly open. I suddenly realize where: in the movie *Willard*. And it's not squirrels; it's rats. Now they are pouring out of the trees, a whole pack of them, moving like one huge collective rat. Later, I found out that this is why you seldom see homeless people sleeping in the park. They are terrified of the rats. News flash: so are we.

Good thing that I'm not a gambler, because I would have bet the farm that we'd be abducted by aliens long before we'd be attacked by rats. But it is definitely happening. They are making a noise that sounds like a collective war whoop. I catapult myself off the bench. Bad move, because when I do that and everything's not quite "reconnected," I can't support myself. As soon as I get up, I'm down again, flat on my face. Crutches bite into my arms, and everything gets badly scraped.

Now we're all moving faster than greased lightning. Hester and three of the Angels grab me and try to haul me to my feet. The others are kicking and flailing away at the rats with anything at hand. Everyone's screaming. The Angels would rather be facing armed drug dealers, and Hester and I would definitely cast our votes for the alien abduction scenario. Anything but the rats. Forget the backpacks and gear on the bench. We'll retrieve them after the rats leave. If the rats leave.

I am terrified that I am going to be bitten by rats as Hester and the Angels struggle to get me on my feet. Finally vertical, I am still unable to navigate. They drag me away from the madness, and an Angel named Bigfoot gets down on one knee and has me sit on his other leg. I start taking inventory. I'm banged up and scraped but have no rodent bites or serious injuries. The rest of our group has also survived, shaken but apparently unharmed.

It's not too long before the absurdity of the situation strikes us. I'm still perched on Bigfoot's knee, and he asks me if I've been a good little girl all year. Entering into the spirit of the thing, I tell Santa what I want for Christmas: a truckload of rat poison. He says that good little girls shouldn't be out here in the middle of the night posing as rat food. At this point, everyone gets in on the act. There is a rat-squealing contest and plenty of tasteless dead-rat jokes. Soon we are doubled up with laughter. Everything is going to be all right, although I must admit that we retrieve our abandoned packpacks with the utmost care. And that is the last time we ever stop on those benches.

Year after year, it is inevitable that someone new to our marathon family will make the logical suggestion of a break on the park benches at Eighty-ninth Street. It is then that the whole group recoils in mock horror and the saga of "The Great Rat Attack" is recounted in all its hideous splendor. With each annual retelling, the rats seem to grow larger and the battle more fierce. Even those who were not there for the original incident remember it as if they were. Such is the magic of tribal storytelling. Such is the power of legend.

OVER THE YEARS, through moments of heart-pounding terror and all the long, cold hours spent pushing through the night, the Angels have taught me about the power of keeping your word. They do not take this yearly pilgrimage of ours casually. At some point during the night, it stops being an adventure. It stops being fun. It's cold. It's danger-ous. It's scary. And still they keep doing it with the same sense of connectedness and purpose with which they started out.

I know that I can always depend on them to help me get where I've gotta go. Their unfaltering dedication makes me want to be the best that I can be along the way. It makes me even more adamant about sticking with the original course and not taking an alternate route. About remaining true to the race, the city, and ultimately to myself.

When you make a promise, as the Angels did, you not only give something of yourself, but you get something very special in return. Many times I have seen them try to cover tears of joy at the finish line. They are moved by our achievement. It matters to them a great deal. They recognize it as their winning moment as well as ours.

They empower me. They inspire me. In daily life, from day to day, they teach me about the power of keeping my word. No matter what.

CHAPTER 6

I NEVER REALLY knew my mother. Not in the classic sense that one knows or remembers a parent. There were no mother-daughter shopping sprees. No heart-to-heart tête-à-têtes. No matriarchal treasure trove of wisdom or witticisms.

As a child, there was only pain and fear. And long after the pain dulled to numbness, the fear remained. As an adolescent, I felt contempt and disillusionment. And as an adult, I knew sorrow and loss for what never was, tempered by the healing balm of time, distance, and acceptance.

I never really did know my mother, but I was intimate with her twin demons: alcohol and drugs. Her life was a macabre ventriloquist act, her every gesture, thought, and deed controlled by forces that she could neither understand nor exorcise. Life included moments of violence and irrationality so profound that, even forty years after the fact, their memory can catapult me back into that primal state of childhood terror and hopelessness. My mother died many years ahead of her time, fearing death and its finality as much as she had feared life and its endless array of choices, chances, and consequences.

If I had to write a requiem for our relationship, it would be a highly personalized paraphrase of the old adage "That which does not kill us can only make us stronger." For not only have I survived my mother in the obituary-based definition of the word, but, much to my credit, I have truly outlived her.

Adversity in its proper framework can be a powerful learning tool. My mother, in her fashion, was probably the quintessential teacher. She was a fully illustrated encyclopedia of who not to be and how not to live your life.

The problem with living life in this default mode is that, while we know all too well what we don't want, we have absolutely no idea of what we do want. We keep hoping that, by the process of elimination, somehow, some way, some of the good stuff will magically show up. As a child, I knew only too well who not to be, and hungered for role models to help me find an answer to what I saw as the most important question of my life: What does it mean to be a woman? Even in elementary school, I understood that certain times and events are important. That the time of the full moon is a time of great power and that becoming a woman would be a watershed in my life.

And then the magical moment finally happened. I was a nine-year-old parochial school student. Tall and gangly and bigger than all the other kids, and I had my first period. It was one of the biggest disappointments of my life. I don't know whether it's that I had some kind of tribal memory, a collective inherited text of the way things used to be when life was closer to nature and the onset of menses was a time of magic and celebration. I thought this would be a time when women would come and tell me secrets of what it is to be female. The only thing I got was a sanitary napkin shoved between my legs.

This didn't work for me at all. Information should have

been passed down to me. And that was why, when I became an adult, I would try to be a source of that information, of the tribal wisdom, to other women. I have always believed in this kind of sharing, not only as a cultural obligation but as an important form of bonding.

But my mother was the product of a strict Victorian-Irish Catholic upbringing, and her relationship to the physical and sexual aspects of life was difficult at best. She told me that I could never ask a man for a box of Kotex, because men don't understand those things. She told me to write him a note and hand it to him in the drugstore. She said that every decent woman does it this way.

"For how long," I asked.

"Until you're old and stop having periods," she answered.

Even at that age, I was absolutely outraged. At first, I couldn't imagine this process, and then, as I visualized it, I realized I was going to have a period every month for something like forty years. So I was supposed to write notes for what? Five hundred or more boxes of sanitary napkins? To me at nine, that was longer than eternity. No way, I decided. This was too important to me. I was a woman and I took it very seriously. It was something of which I was very proud.

If the man in the drugstore couldn't understand the process, then I would explain it to him. I got out my art supplies and made up an elaborate booklet—"I Have My Period"—complete with drawings of all the relevant body parts.

I took it to the drugstore, handed it to the pharmacist, and patiently explained to him everything about the tubes and the uterus and the monthly cycles, ending with my needing a sanitary napkin. I told him that every month I would be coming in and asking for a box of Junior Kotex. My mother said that men don't understand this, I explained. So I made up a this booklet to show everything he needed to know. And now that he understood, I wouldn't have to write him notes for the next forty years.

The pharmacist listened seriously. "You drew all these pictures and wrote all this just for me?" he said with wonder in his voice.

"Yeah," I said.

"Well, I understand it now," he assured me. "And now you don't have to hand me notes. You can just ask me."

No turning back now. I was on a roll. "Maybe," I suggested, "you could keep this book and show it to the other men who work here. Kind of like a reference book. You know, just in case you take a day off when I need a box of Kotex."

He assured me that he would personally make sure that all the men who worked in this store got an opportunity to see the book. He covered his mouth and had what looked like a sudden fit of coughing. Remembering that moment twenty years after the fact, I realized that it was suppressed laughter. What a nice man.

My being the first to get my period was a very big deal with my classmates. But it was not enough to say it had happened. Each girl had to prove it. The way she did this was to pass a used sanitary napkin through the bathroom door to the waiting classmates. When I offered my proof, I was revered. I was so excited that I made up a brand-new edition of "I Have My Period" and brought it to school, along with a clean sanitary napkin, for show-and-tell. After all, this was a miracle of life that everyone should know about. It was a coed class, but I realized that the boys were probably just like the pharmacist. The sooner they learned, the better it would be for everyone. I thought that if they knew how special it was to be a woman, they would stop snapping our bra straps and doing other stupid things to us. It seemed worth a try.

Our nun, Sister Regina, was very sweet about all of this. Although she cut me off the minute she saw the sanitary napkin come out of my lunchbox, she was not unsympathetic. She escorted me into the hall and explained that this was a very private thing that should be kept amongst women, and that the boys in the class would be given the information at home by their mothers and fathers.

I would continue to learn the mechanics of being female, but what it means to be a woman would not come for several years, not till I met what would become my surrogate family and the woman who would be my mentor and fulfill the role of a mother to me.

IT IS SEVEN years later, and I am a junior at St. Michael's Academy on Thirty-third Street between Ninth and Tenth Avenue on the West Side of Manhattan. Life is no easier at home, and that is hard for me. But when I turn sixteen, an avenue of temporary escape presents itself. I am old enough to get a part-time job.

Just a few blocks from the school, right across from Macy's, is Walden's Dress Shop. As soon as I can get working papers, I apply for a job and am accepted. Working is not an absolute financial necessity for me; it's a legitimate reason not to be home. I can work at Walden's after school, thus delaying my return home. It also gives me a reason to leave my Queens home for Manhattan on weekends. I will work my way through high school and college at Walden's.

All I want is a legitimate reason not to go home, but I am to get so much more at Walden's. The staff there is composed of women who are strong female presences. Predominantly, they are the heads of their households. Most of them are women of color from the strong matriarchal tradition of the South. One is the woman who takes me under her wing, Mary.

Mary is twenty-eight years old and seems enormously older than I. To me, she is the epitome of a grown-up. She already has four children and an alcoholic husband who doesn't contribute anything to the household but anxiety. She is the sole source of emotional and financial support for her family. But in spite of all the pressure and responsibilities, she takes me under her wing and always has time for me.

She is to teach me many things that I will carry with me throughout my entire life. The primary lesson is that you can always find equal amounts of evidence to verify that people are either good or bad. Why not make them good?

I remember one particular incident when someone treated her badly in the shop. I was absolutely outraged.

"How can she treat you like that? You didn't do anything to her. How can she be so stupid? God, it's like she's evil. Wait till she comes back to pick up her lay-a-way next week, all smiley, like nothing happened. We'll make her wait. Ruin her lunch hour. Really give her something to act snotty about. We'll get even."

But Mary replied, "You know, my dear, there's just as much reason at any given moment to believe that people are either totally good or totally bad. And the truth is, they're probably neither. Maybe, in the final analysis, it serves us to believe that they're good. At any rate, all they do from moment to moment is the best they can. Maybe it's not always a good job. But that's how life is. If we spend our lives trying to be right or trying to get even, then we don't have a life; we have a scorecard."

Mary teaches me that love tempers circumstances so that you can continue to have a spiritually rich and rewarding life no matter how hard it gets. If you have that as a foundation and a willingness to believe that people are primarily good, your ability to love is unbounded. Her ability to both love and hope have never been compromised by the circumstances of her life, no matter how dire they are. Many people hold out and are willing to feel or to give love only if the setting or circumstances are right. They believe that circumstances create the ability to love. Not Mary.

As a kid, I take it for granted that an older person like Mary has time for me. As an adult, I now realize what kind of emotional investment it must have been for her. She has a difficult life, raising four children essentially by herself, dealing with her husband, trying to make ends meet, trying to make the kids turn out right. Yet whenever I come to her with talk of tests I am studying for or the many problems of a teenage girl, she is there for me, just as she is for her own children. For all intents and purposes, she is my mentor. She is my surrogate mother.

Mary is one of the reasons I have worked with junior and senior high school students whenever I have had that opportunity. It is the way I can best repay Mary for the gifts she gave me. She never allowed circumstances to dictate when and how much she loved. Neither will I. If there is a good karma bank, Mary is a rich woman. A very rich woman indeed.

I begin to learn all of this at Walden's. And while Mary is the woman I am closest to, they all contribute lessons.

There is Miss Rose, an older Jewish woman perhaps in her seventies, who works in the office as the head book-keeper. She is a tough taskmistress, and she teaches me accounting skills and practical business procedures that I will use all my life.

Another elderly woman is Miss Feather. She has a delightfully elaborate hairdo that goes from here to the moon—the original Marge Simpson, except hers is platinum white. Originally of South African English ancestry, she maintains a bit of an accent—just enough to lend a touch of class and a hint of royalty to the most mundane of occasions. With Miss Feather, the luncheon special at Paddy's Clam House is suddenly transformed into dinner at the Waldorf. She teaches me that we invent our own good times by valuing the moment and the people we share it with.

Wilma is Mary's sidekick and works alongside her at the front desk. Every time I am around her I can almost hear a low-frequency hum of contentment; it seems to emanate from the very core of her being. She loves her husband. Loves her life and loves her child. She gives me hope that one day maybe I too can learn to vibrate with the inner sense of peace and joy she seems to possess.

And then there is Elaine, another of the Southern matri-archs, joyous in her essential womanhood. She is the one who notices right away when I come into work terribly depressed. In biology class we are learning about herma-phodites—creatures that are both male and female. Like most girls back then, I don't understand all the parts of the female anatomy. What I do know is that I have a button, and, in the wake of my biology class, I assume this is a small penis. I am completely freaked out, sure I am turning into a hermaphodite.

"Child," Elaine challenges me, "you look like a pile of you-know-what. What's going on?"

"Nothing."

"Oh, yes, there is," she says, not willing to let me stay in a serious funk. She gives me a little shove just to show me she's serious, and repeats her request. "Now you ante up and tell me what's up."

"I'm turning into a man!" I wail. There. It's out, and I am an emotional mess.

"What are you talking about?" she asks.

"Well," I venture, "I've got this thing . . ."

That's enough. She puts her hands on her hips, throws back her head, and laughs a big, honest laugh that shakes her body to the core and brings tears to her eyes. When she catches her breath, she clears things up for me.

"Girl, that ain't nothin' but the boy in the boat," she says. "Someday some man gonna come along and teach that child to sing. Ah-huh!"

I'm not exactly sure what she's talking about, but she keeps on, giving me essential knowledge for the ages. "Many years down the road, you're going to remember this old girl telling you, 'Don't you never take up with no man who can't do more for you than you can do for your-self, child.' " And with that, she dispatches me to the bath-room with specific instructions on what to do about the boy in the boat. I am enormously relieved that I am not turning into a man after all. For all intents and purposes, I am just a normal healthy woman. At least physically.

Over the years, the women in Walden's heal me in ways that they couldn't even begin to imagine. I am a sponge, eager to soak up the things they can teach me. No one at Walden's ever set out purposely to teach me anything. From moment to moment all these women were doing was living their lives and being themselves. And yet there were lessons of inestimable value. Miss Rose taught me the satisfaction of a balanced general ledger and a balanced life. Miss Feather taught me the simple pleasures that can be extracted from the everyday happenings of life. Wilma taught me "humming." Elaine taught me of the joy and personal responsibility of adult sexuality. And Mary taught me about the meaning of faith and the power of love.

At the end of my years at Walden's I am truly well educated, in every sense of the word. But no one knows about my situation at home. Not even Mary. Many years later, I learn that this is not at all unusual. Secrecy and shame are the hallmarks of the dysfunctional family unit. The three-fold mandate that we live our lives by is learned at a very early age. Don't talk. Don't trust. Don't feel.

Long after I am no longer working there, I maintain my contact with Walden's. Then, some years later, an out-of-control car crashes through the display window, running down shoppers, scattering racks of dresses, sending flying glass in all directions. It is a scene of true horror, and I will learn that Mary is in the center of it. She displays enormous courage, helping the wounded, keeping a level head when all about her are losing theirs. In spite of her best efforts, there is one fatality. The accident is so traumatic that Walden's never opens again.

And so I lose track of Mary and all the women who have been so important to the development of my concept of womanhood. The women who have empowered me as a female. But I find their influence does not wane over the years; it grows. So I go through phone books and eventually try a computer search. All to no avail. Then, when I have all but given up hope of finding Mary, I run into her sidekick Wilma—right in the middle of Thirty-fourth Street, a block away from where Walden's used to be. It is a joyous reunion.

It is 1996, and both she and Mary have seen me on TV finishing the marathon and doing the stuff I do in school with kids. Wilma gives me Mary's phone number and, after more than twenty-five years, we are finally reunited.

I call her up and we both cry buckets on the phone. She tells me that it does her heart good to see the difference that I've made in other people's lives, and that she now draws on me as a source of strength when she needs to get through a day. This blows me off the planet, because, even after all these years, I feel it is she who still guides me.

Neither of us, it seems, has had a primrose path through life, but her story tears my heart out. Mary's oldest daughter, Diane, has always been the kind of person to take anyone's lead but her own. She will do anything suggested to her and has no will or internal voice to ground or guide her. Diane has taken up with a bad man, who gives her a beautiful baby and then takes it away, killing the toddler in a fit of drugged-out rage. Diane herself has a drinking problem. She seems unable to separate her destiny from that of her father, who succumbed to the ravages of alcoholism. It turns out to be a self-fulfilling prophecy. Diane, drunk, falls down, hits her head, and dies two days later. Her injuries do not justify her death. Mary believes that she just got too tired to continue the struggle, so she gave up. Her life was not without meaning or legacy, however. She left behind a teenage son. He's a really great kid, warm, intelligent, and loving. And so the best of who she was lives on in him.

Two of Mary's other children have left home and gone about the business of jobs and children and all the trappings of adult lives. They still maintain close family bonds. Mary's youngest daughter, Renee, a wonderful, bright young woman who is the spitting image of Mary, remains at home. Together they raise Renee's daughter and Diane's son.

But although Mary remains as optimistic as ever, the circumstances of her life have taken their toll on her physically. She has already suffered a heart attack and multiple operations on her legs for circulatory problems. In spite of it all, she has continued to work full-time as the supervisor in a nursing home. You can bet that the residents plan their weeks around Mary's work days. She brings them not only care, but love and joy and life.

We get off the phone with an indefinite plan to meet. I am so afraid that this will be just one more thing that gets postponed till it's too late, till one of us has died or moved away again. But later, Renee contacts me and we plot a surprise reunion at their apartment in the northernmost part of the Bronx.

When I arrive, Mary recognizes me instantly, and I her. We fall into each other's arms, bawling like babies, then step back as she holds my face in her strong, protecting hands, looking at me as if I were a long-lost daughter. But now, the twelve years that separate us are no longer an enormous gulf. They are but a few ticks of the clock. In a sense, we are more than mother-daughter now. We are sisters.

At last I am able to tell her what my life was really like and how much she meant to me. She had never realized that I had anything other than a normal adolesence. To say the least, she is dumbfounded. We speak of many things on that winter afternoon, two weeks before Christmas. We talk about old times and the women at Walden's. Many of them have died in the past five or ten years. I shouldn't be surprised, but somehow I am. I guess that when people exist so vividly in the detail and nuance of memory, it's hard to picture them reduced to that primal compound of dust and ash.

Before my reunion with Mary, I had been greatly disturbed to hear the way life had afflicted her. I wished better things for her in the traditional sense of how the world at large interprets those words. Then we meet and I see that she is totally fine: she understands and accepts that tragedy is as much and as vital a part of life as triumph, and that we can not truly have one until we have tasted its opposite.

I know this is true, because I have come to learn that having MS is a burden, but it is also a gift. It is the gift of knowing with certainty that my life has a beginning and an end, that I am truly mortal and will perish. The knowledge makes me stronger and more committed to being fully alive. It forces me to choose life, and from moment to moment to choose consciousness—instead of obliterating the pain and my senses with painkillers and antidepressants.

I ask her where she gets her strength. She tells me that God gives her strength, because she has a purpose in life and her life has meaning. She has that most precious gift of faith, both in her God and in humanity, and sees the things that happen to her as tests. And she believes that time and again she has been given the strength to pass them.

Mary recites a line based on the Bible, the polestar by which she guides her life: "Let my light shine, so that men might see and glorify the Father that is in me."

In classic women's mythology, a woman's life has three stages—the maiden, the mother, and the crone. As I approach my fiftieth year, it is this third and final stage of life that I explore and embrace. Cronehood. It is not a bad word. In fact, quite the opposite. In many tribes, the crone is the wise woman of the tribe, the giver of the laws, the knower of the secrets. She has learned the lessons of both the maiden and the mother and so has become the fulfillment of everything it means to be a woman. She is a revered figure because at any given moment she can embrace and enact any or all of the traditional roles. Mary has understood this instinctively all her life.

And so I still look to Mary as a friend and a mentor, because even as I age, I look to women who are a decade ahead of me to learn how to reach cronehood with grace and with goodness. There will always be something I can learn from her.

Twenty-five years is a long time between meetings, but as I say good bye to Mary and we promise to meet again, I am filled with gratitude. It is truly unusual to be able to come full cycle on such an important part of your life. It's been a gift for me to find her again after all these years. To let her know that all she did hadn't been in vain. To finally get the chance to say thank you, and to let her know that I've turned out OK.

By outside standards, you might look at the logistics and the narrative of her life, and be numbed. Yet she is obviously not just a survivor, but a total winner. A woman who has transcended circumstances to a point where, a quarter-century after the fact, I still consider her a role model.

It's good to know that I have done her proud.

CHAPTER 7

FROM WHERE I stand, the hill, like the Verrazano Narrows Bridge, seems to go on forever. It is a big hill, three miles of country road from the top, where I am now, to the bottom, where I am going. In my mind, it is a mountain. But then again, I do have a tendency from time to time to make mountains out of molehills.

I am in the Catskills in upstate New York, no more than a hundred miles northwest of New York City. It is where I come every year late in the summer for renewal. My time to rediscover things like trees and green growing things and furry animals. My time to play the country kid.

I tend to lose my senses in the city, or at least to turn them off. There is so much noise, I stop hearing. So many sights, I forget to see. So many odors, I don't want to smell. But I get to reclaim them all in the green hills of upstate New York. I get to walk on real grass, and when I do, I remind myself that I am treading on the universe of a thousand unknown creatures who reside in each blade of grass. And I am grateful to them for allowing me to do so.

From the top of the hill, I can smell the rain before it comes. And I can see the lines of storm clouds forming and moving in. Weather is a visceral thing here, and you can participate in it on a very sensory level. In the city, weather is something that happens to you and on you. The skyscrapers close you in, take away your sense of space and distance. In the country, you can actually see how far away the rain is and predict its arrival. Only on the Verrazano Bridge do you get to do that in New York.

My day revolves around the hill. At the bottom is the little town of Woodridge, barely a wide spot on the winding mountainous road. At the top is the Rosemond Hotel, an old-style family resort that offers campsites and cabins. Joe and Lana are the proprietors, and you couldn't ask for more decent, hospitable folks. When I am at the Rosemond, I can eat anything I want, because I'll burn off every calorie and then some on that hill. Every day, I make the round trip to town and back. It is great training for the marathon, which is now just two months away. It is great training—hard training—for the marathon and for life.

Much of the reason I return to the Rosemond every year is this hill—to come back and stand at the top and look down the tree-shaded road that seems to stretch on forever, and then to stand at the bottom, looking up at what always seems an unscalable height. In the ten years I have been coming here, no matter how many times I make the journey up and down my very own mountain, I always have the same thoughts. When I set out, "How will I ever get all the way down?" And on the return trip, "How will I ever make my way back home?"

It is a reminder that all things in life have beginnings, middles, and ends, and that nothing goes on forever. Not the good stuff. Not the bad stuff. Not anything. So I break my journey into stages, with landmarks along the way. I have my knapsack on my back, which I will fill with a day's worth of groceries at the IGA store in town. My Walkman is tuned to a local station that plays terrific oldies. I feel like the happy wanderer.

I first came to this area the year before I started doing the marathon. An ad for a place named the Vegetarian Hotel had caught my eye. I called and asked whether there were all ages and kinds of people there. They said yes, which was true as long as you were talking about all ages over seventy and all different dialects of Hebrew and Yiddish. In some ways, it was more like a club than a hotel, because a good many of the people had been coming here since it was founded, some fifty years earlier.

Initially, I found this very disturbing. I couldn't imagine what I could possibly have in common with these people. Many of them spoke a language with which I didn't even have a nodding acquaintance. Spanish I could fake well enough, but Yiddish was definitely pushing it. And to top it all off, most of the guests were more than twice my age.

I spent that first day roaming around, trying to decide if I could swallow my disappointment or if I should go home and forget about my vacation altogether—lock myself in my air-conditioned apartment and sulk for a week. What the hell.

And then, adjacent to the dining room, I stumbled upon a small sitting room where one entire wall was plastered with pictures. Almost fifty years of the history of the Vegetarian Hotel.

Some photos in black and white depicted family portraits of robust children and proud smiling young parents. Later photos were in faded color, the same couples, now middle-aged and without the children. And sometimes there were even more recent photos of a solitary man or woman, aged and no longer in a couple. Sole survivors of the inevitable losses wrought by time and mortality.

There were photos of birthday parties, anniversary parties, costume parties, and picnics, the identifying dates and inscriptions illegible and almost invisible. Here was a half-century photographic genealogy of one small, summertime community. Still-life cinéma verité at its absolute best. I returned to that wall again and again. For reasons I have never fully understood, it was the wall that made me stay.

Once I was able to put aside my expectations and presuppositions, I realized that this would be a vacation unlike any I had ever had before. Or would probably ever have again.

I began to chat with the other vacationers and found them eager to share their life stories with me. I was a fresh, young audience, more than willing to take the trip down memory lane. And so I became a time traveler, visiting places and historical moments in the lives of my tour guides. I relived with them the universal, basic human stories of births, deaths, loves, and losses, each siphoned through the filter of time, memory, and personal meaning. Each, in its own way, unique, compelling, and totally memorable.

I found at the Vegetarian Hotel not at all what I had expected, but rather an eclectic, artsy group of people. Some of the regulars, when they first started coming to the Catskills, had been naturists, what we now call nudists. That and the whole idea of vegetarianism were very avant-garde at the time. One day, one of the women, who had to be in her eighties, took off the top of her bathing suit as she got into the pool. Physically, she looked like someone out of a *National Geographic* magazine from the 1950s, or maybe a prehistoric figurine of a fertility goddess. No matter how healthy you are, by the time you're in your eighties, gravity is a force that can not be resisted.

But that wasn't what made the moment amazing. Not at all. It was how everyone responded to her. I have never seen such a unanimous male reaction in my entire life. There was nothing lewd or inappropriate about it, but it was something sexual in a real, honest, and appreciative way. She knew how to be sexy, and with that one act of taking off her top, she turned every head in the whole place. All the men within twenty feet, whether it was the college-age busboys or the men her own age, sat up and took notice. No one was grossed out. She vibrated with the radiance of an aging goddess.

And in that act and how she did it, she gave me a strong sense of what adult sexuality is really about. It's that ability to present yourself with grace and pride and, through the projection of your body, to give people a glimpse into your spirit, as well.

Every night, the residents put on their own entertainment programs, frequently old vaudeville skits and comedic *shtick,* a great deal of it in Yiddish. I don't speak a word of Yiddish, but I went to the performances, and the strength and talent of the actors was so great that I could understand through the inflections and gestures exactly what was going on.

One night a much older man took the stage. He had wanted to be a vaudevillian. Back in those days, more than a half century ago, theater and vaudeville were not considered appropriate occupations for people from conservative religious backgrounds. His father, a very devout Jew and a highly respected cantor in their synagogue, forbade him to perform publicly. He was given the choice of expulsion or acquiescence. Like his father, he became a cantor.

He told this story as a preface to his performance. I could

hear the faint traces of longing and regret in his voice, even after all those years. His father was many decades deceased and he himself was many years retired. With a devilish grin, he informed us that he now performed everywhere and anywhere he damned well pleased. And he pleased that night.

His skit was wholly in Yiddish. I understood it as I would have understood if I were in a foreign country hearing a mother yell at her children or lovers cooing to each other. And, as is often true when we listen with our hearts as well as our ears, the universality of the moment transcended the arbitrary boundaries of language.

His performance was sheer magic. People laughed till they cried. As he took his final bow, all smiles and bravura, I suddenly got a lump in my throat the size of a Mack truck. There was something about the look on his face that made me want to cry. It was a look I recognized from times and moments in my own life. It was what I've come to know as the "good-bye look": that long, loving, final look that imprints for all time the indelible memory of people, places, and moments that we don't expect ever to see again. It is the thirsty look that drinks in all the associated colors, sounds, and emotions and stores them in the warehouse of memory. That sacred space to which each of us holds our own magical key. It is the lingering glance we give from the back of a speeding train, long after the station house and all we have left behind have become mere specks in the distance. This is the "good-bye look."

Later in the evening, I went up to him to say thank you. The lump in my throat was back and I found I could hardly speak. He had the wisdom to recognize my distress and to identify its probable cause. "It's OK," he said, giving me a quick hug. "I've had a long life and a good life. I think that this may very well be my last summer. And I guess that would make this my farewell performance. I'm glad for one more chance to make people happy and see them laugh. Keep it as a parting gift."

My instincts were right, but there was no comfort in the knowledge.

Every night brought a new experience for me and a new opportunity for everyone else. Once a week, as part of the entertainment, there were classes in ballroom dancing. To the hotel regulars, the instructors were like gods, the ones everyone stood back to watch in awe on the ballroom dance floor. In reality, they were just average dancers, but they brought such energy and life to what they did that they were totally infectious. Under their excellent tutelage and approving eye, even the clumsiest and least talented of their students became Fred Astaire and Ginger Rogers. If only for that moment.

Another night, they brought in a group of Afro-American and Hispanic kids who were staying at a nearby summer camp, run by one of the major drug rehab centers in the city. The kids were there to sing. The people who came to the Vegetarian Hotel had led culturally sequestered lives, insulated by culture, language, ethnicity, and their neighborhoods from contact with people different from themselves. To them, these kids were as different as they could be. They were people of color, a group with whom the hotel residents had had little, if any, contact during their lives. Worse, from the residents point of view, they had come from a drug rehabilitation program, a scary prospect in and of itself. So the residents sat nervously, unsure of how to react—and so not reacting at all.

One kid in particular sensed the uneasiness of the moment more than the others. He understood that it didn't matter who he was or how well he performed, he would not be accepted. With his two young female companions humming backup, he did a superb a capella rendition of the Whitney Houston song "The Greatest Love of All."

It seemed that the more he sensed the wall between his world and that of his audience, the more of himself he put into his song. Finally his voice took flight, completely free and strong and beautiful. Soaring over the barriers in the room, over the small-town confines of Woodridge, and reaching, reaching, reaching into the universe. He put his very soul into that song, and at the end, his magnificent effort was rewarded with sparse, polite applause. He didn't seem to mind at all. He didn't even appear to notice. I believe that ultimately he had sung the song for himself, as a validation of his hopes and a commitment to his future. And that was all that really mattered.

I have a "healing book" that I discharge energy and prayers into at the end of my day. Even though I never knew his name or where he lived or what brought him to that rehab program so long ago, he's still in my book. I pray that the power he had in his voice has manifested itself in his life. And to this very day, every time I hear that song, I remember him and his moment of triumph, and I fall apart.

BY THE MIDDLE of the week, I must admit, I was getting kind of antsy. My interest in ballroom dancing had reached an all-time low, and there's only so much vaudeville I could take, no matter what language it was in. Also, there was only so much healthy food I could eat in one week; I would have killed for a slice of pizza and a Coke. So I wandered around the surrounding area in search of whatever adventure was to be had, culinary or otherwise.

It was on one of these mini-quests, about a quarter of a mile away, that I found the Rosemond. They had sites for camper-trailers as well as simple cabins. On the weekends, they brought in a disc jockey, and on Friday nights there was a movie. It was owned by a couple who were the second generation of their family to run the place. I made arrangements to stay there the following year, and I've gone back every year since. I like to think of it as a Club Med for people of very modest means.

When I'm at the Rosemond, I keep my own schedule, away from telephones and alarm clocks. A couple of people back home have a number where I can be reached in an emergency, but that's it. Everyone and everything else can just wait. At some point I realized that the universe is not going to fall apart if I abdicate for a week. Hard to believe, but it's true. That's a basic truth most of us have to learn. The world was here before me and it will probably be here long after I'm gone.

I leave a trunk up there, with a small black-and-white TV and a brightly colored tablecloth. When I get off the bus from New York in Woodridge, I do my major grocery shopping for the week at the IGA and take a cab to the hotel. It is after Labor Day when I arrive, and all the vacation folks have gone home. I like it best then, when it's quiet and I have an opportunity to think. It also backs into my birthday and my religious rituals surrounding that time. I don't have to be on anyone else's agenda or meet anyone else's demands. I do many things up here, including nothing at all.

My days are what I decide they will be. I bring up a lot

of books to read, because having the time and luxury to crawl into a book is my idea of heaven on earth. Some days I get up really early, pull on my old, tatty bathrobe, get my special tea mug, and make myself a cup of raspberry tea, just the way I like it. Then I crawl out on the porch, cradling the tea for warmth in the chill morning air, and watch the sun come up. It's before the rest of the world is fully awake; just birds waking up and broadcasting revelry to each other and doing whatever it is that birds do to get their days moving. Basically, I just take it all in. Watching nature's shift change. It's as if one shift communicates with the other as they turn the world over for yet another day.

Sometimes I go into the woods and sit in the lotus position, or some reasonable facsimile, and wait for the deer to come. If I am patient, after a while they understand that I don't present a danger to them, and they come near. Not close enough to pet, but close enough to keep me company for a while. But in recent years, that is another small pleasure that exists only in memory, for now there is Lyme disease.

Many of my encounters with wildlife tend to have that element of shock and amazement. Like the time I was bopping down the road, singing along to the oldies coming through my headphones, as tuned out for that moment as I would be on Fourteenth Street in New York City, and I walk right into a raccoon.

The raccoon was minding his own business, doing what I suppose raccoons do—fishing lunch out of someone's garbage can. I thought him to be a handsome fellow. He actually looked just like the cartoon raccoons that, until that moment, had been my entire association with the species. He was standing there on his hind legs, foil-covered treat in hand, just munching away, when I blundered into him. He looked at me and I at him. Then he shrieked, threw his hands up over his head, and his mouth flew open in what looked like surprise. I shrieked, threw my hands up over my head, and stood there with my mouth hanging open. He recovered first, having more experience with humans than I had with raccoons, and went back to his lunch. I put my headphones on again and went back to my road work.

Every trip to town brings new possibilities, new adventures. About halfway into town is a bridge over a creek. I hang over the side, looking for snapping turtles, squirrels, frogs, anything that qualifies as wildlife. I'm not fussy. I'm not proud. I'm not real particular. I'm from the city. I take what I can get.

I keep track of time and distance by the dogs that bark in the houses I pass. After all these years, I know them by their barks, and I listen for every one of them. Sometimes, a dog's voice is lost and I am left to ponder what happened to it.

What I didn't know was that the people who live in those houses listen too. Not for dogs, but for the Zoe creature who comes down the road every year about the same time, singing Golden Oldies at the top of her lungs. I found this out one year when I came a week or two later than I usually do, and some of the locals stopped when they saw me and told me they were afraid I had stopped coming.

The town is not a lot. Blink and you miss it. As in the rest of America, most of the local commerce has moved out to a mall. In Woodridge itself, there's the IGA and Rashkin's Drugstore, where you can get prescriptions filled and over-the-counter medicines and basic stuff. There's a post office, a deli, and few more odds-and-ends shops. And there's my favorite stop of all, the Woodridge Family Restaurant, where they have a great breakfast special that by New York City standards costs just about nothing.

On this particular day, I am headed for the restaurant, just beyond the IGA supermarket. It is early, and I haven't eaten. I'm so focused on the breakfast special that I can taste the eggs. Now I know how my dog feels when she sees that can of food come out of the cupboard.

I am less than a hundred feet from breakfast when almost out of nowhere he jumps into my path. He's probably in his late sixties or early seventies. Judging from the look on his face, he's in a really funky mood. He's dressed in khaki pants, a blue shirt, and white belt and shoes. Perhaps he's in search of a golf ball, or maybe he's just lost one. I have no idea. At any rate, he's a man with a major attitude.

"Goddamn!" he shouts at me. "It's you."

"Nope," I reply, "not me. Definitely not me." I have no idea what he's talking about, but like any good New Yorker I figure I already know what his problem is. He's obviously nuts.

"No," he insists. "It's you. You're Zoe. It is you. I'd know you anywhere."

His name is John, and he proceeds to tell me a remarkable story about how seriously I had ticked him off over the years. John would turn on his television set or open his newspaper and see me, and it always coincided with his being sick or having a serious problem or getting bad news. He really believed that I was a bad omen in his life.

The first time he saw a picture of me, it was in something he was reading in his doctor's office. It was then he learned that he had a heart problem and that maybe he could control it through diet and exercise. Somehow, he connected me to his heart. He decided I was a total jerk. Because here I was running this race and someone was writing about it and as far as he was concerned, it made no difference to anyone on the entire planet. "She's still got multiple sclerosis," he decided. "She's still gonna die. What has she got to look so goddamn happy about?"

He's telling me all this and I'm listening, not having any idea where it's going.

The next time he sees me is the following year on TV, just after he's started having angina attacks and has to carry nitroglycerin pills. Now he's really ticked off. My race makes even less sense to him than the year before. "Writing about you once was forgivable," he says. "You had your adventure, your fifteen minutes of fame, and that should have been the end of it. Give it a rest, already."

So another year comes and goes and now he finds out that if he doesn't change his ways, he's definitely headed for a by-pass—if a heart attack doesn't get him first. He sees me again and he's infuriated. In his mind there is no question that I am the world's biggest jerk and a hopeless moron.

Now it's year number four, and he has just survived a quadruple by-pass. In spite of himself, he looks for me on TV the day after the marathon. He doesn't see me anywhere. Suddenly, he has trouble breathing. "I was afraid that you had either died or given up," he says to me. "And I finally understood that if either one of those things was true, my life would never be the same again, because some part of me would die with you."

John hadn't realized how much of his psychic energy he had invested in my finishing. Two days later, he had his wife call up Road Runners and pretend she was me, calling to check on my time. He found out that it had taken me more than twenty-seven hours to finish the race. "At that point," he says, "I realized that I was out of excuses in my life. I started walking every day. I changed my diet, lost a lot of weight. And here I am, better than ever."

He says that the thing that always got him on TV was my eyes. That he could see genuine pleasure in my face. And he says that he always knew that he would meet me. He didn't know where or when, but he knew that he would. And now that he has, I look exactly as he had expected. I am just who he expected me to be. Eyes and all.

It isn't the kind of situation where we're meant to exchange phone numbers and start sending each other Christmas cards. That would be a forced kind of intimacy. It isn't like that, but rather a moment in time that will last both of us forever. He has given me a treasure from who he is and the sacred place where he lives. And that's all it was ever meant to be.

I think that maybe this is the new definition for intimacy in the 1990s. Ships not passing but colliding in the night, leaving dents and paint scrapes and then steaming on. So many moments in my life have been like that, sacred while they are in progress, but not meant to last forever.

The amazing thing is that John doesn't even live in Woodridge. He lives somewhere in Queens, the borough where I grew up. And the reason that we met at all is that I had decided to come to town early for the breakfast special and he was driving through to somewhere farther upstate, and picked that place and time to get out of his car and buy a can of soda. But other than that and his name—John—I know nothing about him.

I have a strong belief in *synchronicity*. Most people probably think that the world runs by happenstance, accident, and coincidence. I think that perhaps there is not so much a master plan as a master puzzle somewhere, and that things happen far less by coincidence than we suspect. Bit by bit, whether we know it or not, the pieces of the puzzles that constitute our individual lives fall into place. At any given moment, I strongly suspect, we're doing exactly what we're supposed to be doing.

The incident with John is a big reminder of that for me. I may not understand or always appreciate the logistics of my daily life. But I do believe that I'm probably learning exactly what I'm supposed to be learning, so it's important for me to remain conscious and alert in my life. If I am present and accounted for, then every moment brings the opportunity to live and to grow. And every day offers an endless source of adventure and entertainment, whether it's appearing on a national TV show or meeting a raccoon for the very first time in Woodridge, New York.

Again, in part, I think this is one of the gifts of having MS, the knowledge that there is a possibility that my moments are limited, so I had better pay attention. Some people can face the exact same situation and get the exact opposite message. They turn themselves into major drama queens and kings, and what they are really doing is ending their lives long before they die. I look at it the other way. From moment to moment, there's a lot of opportunity. A lot to be grateful for. A lot to look forward to.

That doesn't mean that I don't have days and moments when I don't want to know about anything. We all do. It's part of being human. That's why I have headphones—for days when I want to tune the world out because there's just too much of it and not enough of me to get through the day. From time to time, everyone needs to do that.

The way I try to look at it is not as tuning the world out, but revitalizing. That's my week in Woodridge. There, I don't have to be part of anyone else's agenda. There's no schedule. I can put on my headphones or crawl into a book. I have no demands to meet except my own. Sometimes I work. Sometimes I play. Sometimes I do absolutely nothing. And sometimes, I stand on top of my hill, look down at the road reaching for forever, and wonder what is meant to happen today.

CHAPTER 8

WHEN I SEE people in New York doing things that irrevocably mark them as tourists, I have absolutely no shame. None whatsoever. I walk right up to them and tell them exactly what they're doing wrong.

"Excuse me. Stop doing that. You look like a tourist. You may as well put a MUG ME sign on your back."

Or, "Excuse me. Put the damned camera away. You're asking for someone to tear it off your shoulder and keep going."

I'm brazen because I really like tourists and I don't want them to have a bad experience in my city. Other people have shown me such kindnesses in other cities, particularly with my being on crutches. So whenever I see people who look as if they're setting themselves up for unwanted drama, I step right in. Uninvited and unannounced. I'm a real busybody that way.

There's an old saying that "a friend is someone who knows all about you and loves you anyway." Perhaps the same can be said of our relationship to home towns. With all its quirks and perks and ups and downs, I still love New York. I probably should know better, and I'm glad I never will.

As a native New Yorker, I pride myself on being able to "go with the flow." I'm used to dealing with surprises and accustomed to facing adversity with aplomb.

So what am I doing in a Scranton, Pennsylvania, hotel room totally freaking out over a television set?

I am in Scranton at the invitation of the Reverend Jo Ann Germershausen, the associate pastor of the Covenant Presbyterian Church. It all started after the 1993 New York City Marathon. Wayne Coffey, of the *New York Daily News,* wrote a feature story about me that really captured what my race is all about. The Reverend Jo Ann happened to buy the national edition of the *Daily News* the day the article was in it. She spotted the story about me on her way to work. Once she began to read the article, she started to cry and couldn't stop.

My story struck a chord, because Jo Ann had been widowed early in her adult life, and between raising two children and her ministerial duties, she felt she had run a marathon every day of her life. And now she was reading about someone who really understood what it was like. She read the article again, and then decided that I was going to come to Scranton. Her intention was for me to speak at a Youth Summit they were planning under the auspices of the Points of Light Foundation. The summit also coincided with Heritage Sunday, which would be an opportunity for six or seven churches to come together at Jo Ann's parish to celebrate their Presbyterian heritage. It became her mission to track me down and get me to come to Scranton for that particular weekend.

She preached a sermon about me, talking about survival and determination and following your path no matter what, using the newspaper article as a reference point. Meanwhile, she continued to try to find me, which isn't easy, since I don't have a listed phone number. Finally, after three months of searching and praying, she managed to get in touch with Achilles to tell her story and ask for help. They took her number and passed it on to me.

Jo Ann wasn't home the day I called, and her daughter Katie answered the phone. When I told her who I was, you would have thought a national holiday had been declared in Scranton. The family felt as if their efforts had finally been rewarded and their prayers finally answered.

I left my number, and Jo Ann called me back, almost immediately, her voice filled with excitement. We began to talk and there was an instant bond between us. She told me about the Youth Summit and Heritage Sunday and invited me to attend.

"I know I'm being pushy," she said, "but it would mean so much to us if you could come here and talk to the kids and also to my congregation. I really believe you have so much to share with all of us."

The parish isn't wealthy, but she offered to pay for my bus fare, my meals, and a hotel room. I took two vacation days from work so that I had time to make the trip on the appointed weekend.

And that is how, after a six-hour bus ride and a full day spent at the Youth Summit, I came to be in this hotel room in Scranton about to lose my cool. All my New York education never included a course in hotels. The only time I sleep somewhere other than my own bed is when I go for my annual vacation in the Catskills, and then I stay in a Spartan room with no phone or amenities of any kind. Being in a real hotel was pretty exciting.

My theory about hotels, at least at that point in my life, was that if you don't want me to push the buttons, don't put them where I can reach them. The phone in this place was loaded with extra buttons, so I started pushing them

just to see what would happen. When people started showing up at the door to pick up my dry cleaning and bring
more towels, I decided I'd better stop. Especially since I
had plenty of towels and didn't have any dry cleaning to
take out.

Then, I turned my attention to the television, which was
seriously cool. It had this really impressive remote control
which provided access to about a zillion channels. So I
started flipping all around the dial, getting menus and stations and bulletin boards and the local weather. All of a
sudden I get these two people on my screen doing something that had me thinking, "Where have I seen this before?" And a half beat later, "Oh, so *that's* what they're
doing!" And it's something they definitely shouldn't be
doing in my room. As a matter of fact, they really ought to
be sequestered somewhere behind locked doors and
opaque venetian blinds. As I attempted to get them off my
screen, I marveled at their flexibility and wondered if they
had a good chiropractor. Maybe they were contortionists?
I don't know about you, but such an Olympic-caliber performance would probably land me in traction for at least
six months.

At that point another thought suddenly struck me. This
was a pay-per-view movie—what if the Covenant Presbyterian Church got billed for *Debbie Does the Western Hemi-
sphere and Parts of Asia?* They would surely wonder what
kind of person they entrusted their kids to all weekend. I
would have turned it off anyway, but now I was *really anxious* to get it off my screen. At this point, Murphy's Law
reared its ugly head, because the harder I tried, and the
more buttons I pushed, the louder the sound track got.

The TV was now at full, plaster-cracking volume, and I

was totally freaked out. The people in the rooms on either side of me heard the sound effects and started applauding and yelling encouragement through the walls. Finally, the worldwise, street-smart New Yorker regained enough presence of mind to hit the off button. Duh.

I called the desk to let them know what happened and that I didn't want to watch the movie. The next morning I made sure that Jo Ann knew what had happened, just in case it showed up on the bill. Another life lesson of sorts: be a little more circumspect in the future about pushing hotel room or TV buttons.

At the morning services on Heritage Sunday, Jo Ann tells her congregation that very rarely, if ever, does the focus of one's sermon show up in real life, and here I am. This is a real honor for me, to be a part of her congregation's big weekend, to become part of its legend and history. The members set up a room for me in the church parlor, where I show a video of my race and talk to the assembled congregation. It's a packed house, with kids sitting on the floors and adults sitting in chairs or standing against the walls.

I am able to share with them that my marathon has always been a journey of the spirit as much as of the legs and body. This journey of the spirit is the whole concept and basis of my life. I see life as a holistic experience, and have always believed that you do everything as much with your heart and soul as with any other part of your being. The marathon has become both a physical and metaphysical expression of this belief. It exists as both a race and as metaphor for discipline, self-acceptance, achievement, and ultimately for life itself.

Throughout the weekend, I am both the teacher and the student. I begin to understand, through my participation in the Youth Summit and in Heritage Sunday, that we are all part of a great spiritual continuum. We are a circle with no beginning and no end, all participating in the unique and individual expression of the same ultimate truth.

I was raised in traditional Roman Catholicism, and I respect the Catholic faith. But as it was practiced when I was young, and with the unique realities thrust upon me by my childhood, it was not a workable faith for me. It was based too much on suffering, and I was suffering enough. I realized that religion needs to be joyous.

Yes, part of worship is about taking inventory and trying to live better and to improve yourself. It's following the commandment "Do unto others what you would have them do unto you." There have always been and will always be higher spiritual principles. That's a timeless truth. But there's no reason why truth and joy should be mutually exclusive.

I can give more praise to God while training in the park with my headphones on than I can sitting numbly listening to someone talk about Hell and eternal damnation. I know that Catholicism has changed its focus over the years, but after my experience with it when I was young and my later association with the Foundation, I kind of invented my own thing.

I hold my birthday as a religious holiday, because I don't take it for granted from year to year that I have some special license to live on the planet. Life is a contract that's up for renewal every year right before my birthday. And I renew it diligently with my higher power every September. It is a special part of my annual cycle of retreat and renewal that takes place on my vacation in Woodridge.

I make two lists: one is a wish list and the other is a

thank-you list. I take them out into the woods and burn them. As they burn, I offer back my life for another year, asking for the strength and grace to pursue what's on my wish list and giving praise and thanks for everything I've been given. For all the years of my adult life, my thank-you list has included Mary, and this year that thank you will be for having had the privilege and joy of seeing her again.

That sense of not taking things for granted is very important to me. It is one of the gifts that MS has given me over the years, the certain, irrefutable knowledge that nothing in life is a given. Nothing is forever. It can all be snatched away from us in an instant.

If you have any difficulty believing this, just come to an Achilles Track Club workout and look around. You'll meet people whose lives have been altered forever, frequently for no apparent reason. Accident or crime victims who give new meaning to the idea of being in the wrong place at the wrong time. Others who were left permanently impaired by opportunistic infections, or rare diseases with unpronounceable names, or just your garden variety stroke or bout with cancer.

So I don't take anything for granted. Not the ability to walk. Not the ability to see. Not anything. My vision is fine now, but with MS, at any time I could lose all or part of it. And so I inject as much color as I can into my life. So much, in fact, that my friends accuse me of being a human Crayola box. I take that as a compliment. For if someday it were all taken away from me, without so much as a moment's notice, I want to remember what life looks like. And I want to remember well enough to make it last for a lifetime, if need be.

In addition to my birthday, the equinoxes and solstices

are also days of great religious significance for me. Like just about everyone else, I seem to spend an inordinate amount of time bitching and moaning about the seasons and the weather. So it seems only fitting and fair that I attempt to balance the scales and seek out ways to honor these quarterly changes. Over the years, the solstices and equinoxes have become powerful reminders of the inexorable, unrelenting passing of the seasons, both on the planet and in my life. They've come to represent a quarterly opportunity to realign my personal transformational journey with the larger journey of the world as manifested through the seasons.

On the summer solstice, I try to get to a body of water, whether it's a day trip to Atlantic City or four blocks from my house to the East River. I write out a message—sometimes a wish for the universe, sometimes an anonymous story about where I've been for the year, and sometimes just a poem—and seal it in a bottle. No signature. No return address. And I throw it into the surf and watch it drift away. Maybe someone will find it. Maybe not. But if it's meant to be found, whoever makes the discovery will either think it's very charming or very crazy, or perhaps something more. Maybe it will wake something up inside of the discoverer that hasn't participated in ritual in a long time. Maybe it will bring that person back into the circle. I don't know, and I make it up as I go along.

Others may not agree, but I consider myself a deeply religious person. Some may argue that I can't be, because I'm not born again. But I am born again. I'm born again every single day of my life, and sometimes from moment to moment.

Although I show up at Heritage Sunday with a fair

amount of personal religious doctrine firmly entrenched in my daily life, there are still valuable lessons for me to learn. The weekend gives me an opportunity to rethink the power of traditional religion. When it's used with positive focus, and put into action in the form of community programs and real caring, it's a mighty force to be reckoned with.

Jo Ann's community is a shining example of real commitment to youth. All the programs are based on the implicit understanding that youth needs not only to move away from the enslavement of drugs and alcohol, but needs to move toward something as well. And in pursuit of this all-important outcome, the members have invited me into their lives and have graciously hosted my weekend in Scranton.

I talk a great deal with Jo Ann on that trip, and despite our different approaches, we have far more in common that we have differences. It is apparent that we have formed a bond that will last the rest of our lives.

Before I leave, she and many of her parishioners make a commitment to come to New York for the annual MS Walk-a-thon. They keep their promise, boarding a bus at five A.M. in Scranton to get to New York in time for the walk. Some of them work shift jobs and have stayed up all night to do this. They are not by any means wealthy, but they donate what little money they do have to MS and to pay for the trip.

Even after the walk, they are still so full of life that they have the energy to go sightseeing in the Big Apple. We visit St. Patrick's Cathedral and Rockefeller Center and do all the touristy, fun things that people do when they come to the city.

This is New York, my hometown, and it is my chance to show my friends the city I know and love. The things I take so for granted are as foreign to them as that hotel room in Scranton with all its buttons and gewgaws was to me. The city, by reputation, is a daunting and dangerous place. For those of us who live there, it's home. While it's true that you have to keep your wits about you, it's nowhere near as dangerous as what the tabloids would have you believe.

There is payback for me in playing tour guide. Normally, I never see the tourist sights that everyone visits when they come to New York. I hadn't been to the Museum of Natural History for ages before they came. I hadn't taken the time to drive around town in a bus, gawking out the windows at the shops, the architecture, my fellow citizens in all their motley glory. As much as I believe in not taking anything for granted, I began to realize how caught up I become in my everyday routine, and how much of my life runs on autopilot in this, one of the greatest cities in the world.

So wherever we go and whatever we do, we have a front row seat for the greatest sport in the world—people watching—in this, its greatest emporium. When the folks from Scranton go home, they have a different view of New York, and, to tell the truth, so do I. For them, it is no longer a dark and dangerous place: Sodom and Gomorrah on the Hudson. It is a vibrant and wonderful city, maybe not someplace they want to live, but certainly no longer a place they feel nervous about visiting. For myself, I am reminded that the possibilities for learning and growth and adventure are never more than a subway or bus ride away.

Participation in the MS Walk has become pretty much

an annual event for my friends from Scranton, and also a welcome opportunity to spend time with Jo Ann. As time passes, my respect for Jo Ann has grown by leaps and bounds. She is a warm and wise woman, a person who understands both the ways of the world and the ways of the church. She has a real understanding of what people need. She knows when to listen, when to speak, and when to advise.

If there is a better definition of what makes a good pastor, I haven't heard it.

CHAPTER 9

TWO WOMEN STAND on the curb on Fourth Avenue in Brooklyn, on a day so warm and muggy that you would swear that there is no way it could be November. It is a fine day for watching the multitudes pound by on their way to Central Park and the finish line of the 1993 New York City Marathon.

One of the women had ambitions of being an athlete herself. Her name is Juanita, and until six months ago she had been training to participate as a wrestler in the Gay Games to be held in June 1994. But now it appears that the injuries she sustained in a car accident have crushed these hopes forever. So she stands on the curb with her life partner, Pat, and watches. And she remembers what she has lost.

It is a grand and thrilling scene—the lead runners flashing by and then a trickle of runners that gradually turns into a stream, and then a river, and finally a flood that fills the street and washes against the curb. As Juanita looks up the avenue at the onrushing horde, she sees a woman, with a fringed shawl over her shoulders, moving slowly on two crutches. Her face is pale and sweating and her breathing is labored.

I am oblivious of Juanita and Pat, oblivious of just about everything. The heat and humidity have caught me by surprise, and I am not coping well. In the best of circumstances, my MS and humidity are a bad combination, but at least during the summer, I am conditioned for it. Now, in November, I am ambushed by the unexpectedly muggy day, and my body cannot deal with it efficiently. All morning I have been taking clothes off and putting clothes on, unable to strike the balance that will keep my body temperature at a comfortable level. Although the race isn't even a quarter done, I have already expended far more effort than is normal or appropriate.

Juanita watches me and points me out to Pat. "What's with that woman?" she asks. "She's never going to make it."

Pat looks up and vaguely recognizes me from a story she saw somewhere. "Don't worry," she tells Juanita. "She's gonna do it. She's done it before. I read a story about her. She'll make it."

"Uh-uh. No way is she going to make it," Juanita protests. "Look at her. She's pitiful. Ready to drop any minute."

Pat tells her that the woman with the shawl will make it. Again Juanita tells her, "No way!" The argument goes back and forth as I pass them and slowly disappear, swallowed up by the tide of faster runners. At last, when there is no longer anything to watch, Juanita and Pat go back to Juanita's apartment. Already Juanita has forgotten about the woman with the crutches, forgotten about the runners, forgotten about the marathon.

Whether I make it or not means nothing to her. She really doesn't care who finishes and who doesn't. Once in her life she would have, but not now—not since the accident. She has even stopped going to her physical therapy sessions, doesn't particularly care if she ever gets back on her feet. She has basically surrendered, hauled up the white flag, and waved it at life.

She is thirty-six years·old and more often than not feels like a tired old woman. Her life has never been easy, and there's nothing to make her believe it will ever get any better.

Juanita was a child of the Deep South, the granddaughter of two well-respected Pentecostal ministers. From the time she was a very young girl, she realized that her sense of sexuality was far different from that of other girls her age. Without a doubt, she was attracted to women, an attraction that left her with a great sense of fear and shame. In the language of her culture, there is no place for the word *homosexual*. It is synonymous with the word *abomination*.

Determined to lead a conventional life, she married and gave birth to her first child when she was fourteen. She named him Clay. By the time she was sixteen her daughter Heather had also been born. When asked in later years what her husband was like, she would shake her head with a sad smile and say, "At seventeen, he was all that he could be." The marriage was history by the time she turned eighteen.

At the age of twenty, with a four-year-old and a six-year-old in tow, she moved to New York to live with her mother, who had agreed to help with child care and the endless round of responsibilities involved in maintaining a good home for two small children. Juanita returned to school and got her high school diploma. Shortly after graduation she pursued her bachelor's degree in business administration.

Those were busy and troubled times for her. She felt unable to escape the negative stereotype image of the black woman—teenage mother, and began to drink. Alcohol also provided solace for her complicated feelings about her sexuality. Even as she worked to become upwardly mobile, her nights were filled with low self-esteem and addiction.

In 1987, she met Pat, and although they began a life together, she was still troubled by her sexuality and continued to drink. In 1991, her grandfather and his traveling ministry visited New York to participate in a Pentecostal healing service. In the laying-on-of-hands portion of the ceremony, she approached him and asked him to pray with her for the healing of her sexuality. He sent her back to her seat without so much as a reassuring touch or even a prayer. She believed his message was that she was damned for all eternity, totally beyond salvation. She began to believe that all was lost.

Her drinking escalated until she realized that alcohol was destroying her life; she couldn't live with it and she couldn't live without it. So she decided not to live at all. She took a full bottle of sleeping pills and washed them down with a quart of vodka. She was saved by her therapist, who called her because of a missed appointment. She had forgotten to unplug the phone, and picked it up on pure reflex action. It's ironic how the ordinary auto-pilot actions of everyday life can either save us or damn us. Her therapist summoned the police, and she was rushed to intensive care, where her life was saved.

After the suicide attempt she joined AA and, in the process of getting sober, began to reclaim her life. She also made the career decision to commit her time and talents to the field of nonprofit institutions, where she felt she could really make a difference. She began to come to terms with her sexuality and started training for the Gay Games that were to take place in New York in the summer of 1994.

Her training was both an affirmation of her sobriety and a hallmark of her acceptance of herself as a lesbian woman. For the first time in a long time, life looked pretty good. She was sober, in a good relationship, and was finally doing something in the world that she felt would make a difference.

Then came June 1993 and the car accident that left her neurologically damaged. Her symptoms were not unlike those of MS. Her coordination, balance, and memory were all affected. The cartilage in her left knee was so damaged that she required months of physical therapy. She was told that not only would she never participate in sports again, but would never be able to re-enter the workforce. It was bluntly suggested that she apply for permanent disability benefits.

In the face of this, she lost all hope and fell into a deep depression, wondering if the tacit message of her grandfather was right: maybe she *was* damned. Maybe, in spite of her best efforts, she would never accomplish anything in her lifetime. Maybe this was the punishment for the choices she had made, for the life she led.

Now it was Tuesday morning, two days since Pat dragged her outside to watch the runners. Juanita picks up the newspaper and leafs through it, a daily half-hour diversion from the problems that consume her life these days. A picture and story in the sports section stop her cold. It is the same story, written by Wayne Coffey, that the Reverend Jo Ann in Scranton will also read and respond to.

She recognizes the face from the crowd on Fourth Avenue: the woman on crutches. It took her twenty-eight hours to finish her sixth marathon. But finish she did. And the woman's name is Zoe. Zoe Koplowitz.

Juanita reads the story again and stares at the picture. The story burrows down inside her and finds that tiny part of her that still holds fast to the dream. It breathes new life into her. New determination. She cuts out the article and hangs it over her bed. And she decides that not only is she going to compete in the Gay Games, but she is going to win a gold medal.

When she hangs the picture of me over her bed, she has absolutely no idea who I am. So she makes me up. She looks at my achievement and tries to figure out who I must be and what I must have going for me. What is it that, year after year, gets me to the finish line? Faith. Intensity. Determination. Humor. All of them seem distinct possibilities.

Somewhere in the back of her mind, she realizes that these attributes are in no way foreign concepts to her. She has utilized their strength time and again in the course of her own life, to raise her children, get her education, and make a contribution to the community through her job. She begins to understand that she has to redefine these words of power in the context of her current circumstances. They will weave for her a golden thread, which, when grasped and held tightly, will lead her out of the labyrinth and back onto her path.

Two weeks later, she goes into the gym for the first time in almost six months. It's all she can do to climb the three flights of stairs to sit and watch the other women train. But it's a start. She's back on the team, and that's what really matters.

Every day, Juanita can do a little more, and after two weeks in the gym, she is ready to test her mettle on the road, for without the rigorous aerobic conditioning that running provides, her gym time will become futile. And so, for the first time since the accident, she is going to run.

She gets up early that morning, long before sunrise. All of us who train can identify with her as she reaches into a bag of clean laundry, pulls out a mismatched running outfit, and puts it on. It's 5:30 A.M. as she leaves the apartment. She could start running immediately, but she doesn't. This is not the place to begin her journey back. So she walks to Fourth Avenue and finds the exact spot where our paths had crossed so briefly a month earlier.

This is where she will start, at the place where she began to get her life back. The avenue, lit by streetlights, is still deserted; the city quiet in that eerie, predawn way. Only a garbage truck—a groaning, grinding symphony of metal on metal and growling diesel—breaks the silence. She walks into the street, out to the fading remnants of the blue line that had marked the marathon route.

Up through the soles of her feet, the power of the blue line surges, first into her legs and then into her entire body. Knowing that I, and thirty thousand others, had run on this line before her gives her strength to start over. Tentatively, she moves from a walk to a trot.

In the apartments around her, people are getting up, taking showers, making coffee, getting ready for another day on life's treadmill. There is no one to cheer, no one even to notice as Juanita's trot turns into a run. A month ago, before she ever saw me, she thought she would never have this sensation again. And now she is running on the very same blue line up Fourth Avenue. Emotions wash over her, and as she runs, she sobs with joy, the tears running down her cheeks.

She is able to go just three blocks that first morning, but

she is jubilant and secure in the certain knowledge that this day is the beginning of the rest of her life.

All through the long winter months, Juanita throws herself into her training. Her teammates are so impressed by her dedication and enthusiasm that, when they learn she can't afford the entry fee into the Gay Games, they take up a collection and pay it for her.

The games finally arrive, in June 1994, and they captivate New York, an exuberant panorama of theater and competition. The wrestling event is held in New York University's massive gymnasium. Few if any sports are as physically demanding as wrestling. But the months of hard training pay off for Juanita as she advances to the finals in her weight class.

As she waits for her match, she is a walking adrenaline cocktail, all butterflies and nervous energy. Outside the locker room, the gym is packed with perhaps two thousand spectators, the biggest crowd by far that Juanita has ever competed in front of. Her life partner, Pat, is there. So are her daughter, Heather, and her two grandchildren, Nita and Jonelle.

Before they come to the gym, she tells her family how important it is to her that they are there. She also says that she wants them to know that, no matter what people say about her and no matter what her grandchildren may hear in school about gays, there are some things about her she'd like them to remember. She is a lesbian. She is a good woman. She is a strong woman. All three of these things are true, and none exists in contradiction to the others.

Just before the match is called, she closes her eyes and offers up a prayer to her God. It is not for victory, but rather to have the strength to be the best that she can be. And in her prayer, she invokes the spirits of three of the women of power she has known in her life—her grandmother, her mother, and me. She asks that we will be with her in spirit in this, her greatest moment.

Juanita hears her name called and runs out into a caldron of noise and excitement. But she keeps her focus and wrestles the match she has imagined. She is well ahead on points, and the gold medal is assured, when, with just eight seconds remaining in the four-minute match, she pins her opponent. In front of the most important people in her life, her eyes welling with tears of joy, she mounts the victory stand and accepts her gold medal.

Several days later, the closing ceremonies of the Gay Games are held before more than fifty thousand spectators in Yankee Stadium. As part of the ceremonies, various awards are given out, and Juanita is called to the pitcher's mound to accept the Uncommon Woman Award. The award is given by the Uncommon Legacy Foundation, a lesbian organization that acknowledges significant contributions to society made by lesbian women. The huge crowd celebrates her achievement with a thunderous ovation that takes her so much by surprise, it almost knocks her over. Her pride in receiving the award is her own final recognition and acceptance of her sexuality. Forevermore, whenever moments of darkness and doubt obscure her vision of the future, she will take out her medal and trophy. And she will remember it all.

As you may guess, the story doesn't end here. Not by a long shot. Several days later, the *Maury Povich Show* approaches Juanita and asks her to be part of a program they are doing on the Gay Games. They are touched and intrigued by her story and amazed when she tells them of the newspaper article and the bond she has formed with a woman she has never met. "My life has been saved by a total stranger who doesn't even know I exist," she tells the producers. Maury loves the story, and he and his staff decide to track me down to see if they can have me on as a surprise guest during Juanita's segment.

When they find me and relate the story, I am in awe. There is no other word for it. I am amazed by her achievement and astounded by the part she believes I have played in it.

At this point, however, I am not entirely unfamiliar with the phenomenon. People have walked up to me in the street and told me things like "Hey, I went back to law school after seeing you finish the marathon." Or, "I left a relationship that sucked wind after twenty-five years, and it was all because you gave me the courage to change. So thank you."

I must admit that it bothered me that people seemed to invest an inordinate amount of the decision-making process and their very lives in the strength of something I had done. I could see the connection, but as hard as I tried, I really didn't understand it. Often, I was plagued by moments of paralyzing fear that if people really knew me, and realized I was just an ordinary person, exactly like them, they'd feel cheated, betrayed, let down. And so it was with both excitement and trepidation that I accepted the invitation to be on the *Maury Povich Show* and meet Juanita for the first time.

That was my state of mind as I waited in the dressing room for my cue to go on. Everyone was incredibly excited as they sneaked me in and hid me in another room while Juanita got ready to go on. The producer who had cried when she talked to me on the phone was there, still blown away by the whole story. Pat was there, too, along with Clay and Heather and the grandkids, Nita and Jonelle. All of them knew about the surprise and were having a grand time keeping Juanita from finding out.

When they took her onstage, they let me into the green room so that I could watch while Maury talked to her and began to set things up. She had the newspaper clipping about me that turned her life around. It was tattered and yellowed by then, and she said she had kept it with her from November until now. Every time she thought she couldn't train anymore or couldn't go on for one more day, she would whip out the article, read it, and somehow get the strength to continue.

Finally, they called me onstage. Juanita couldn't believe she was actually meeting me. The emotion of the moment was far more than either one of us could bear, and both of us broke down and cried. Needless to say, there wasn't a dry eye in the studio, and I'm sure the same could be said of the viewing audience at home. And as we talked, and as the show went on, I finally learned the lesson that Juanita was here to teach me, the lesson that so many others have tried to get through to me.

The lesson is that it doesn't matter if I understand what moves and motivates other people. Even now, I don't always get it—I just don't worry about it anymore. The lesson I learned from Juanita is that we can never really know where the Lord or the world will take us. And the best that any of us can do in our lives is to walk our path with an open heart and a willing spirit, believing that in every moment there is an opportunity to make a difference. Whether we recognize it or not and whether we understand it or not, it's always there.

When we believe we can make a difference, we can intend to make a difference. When we intend to make a difference, we can commit ourselves to making a difference. And it is then, when we begin to align our lives with the threefold principles of faith, intentionality, and commitment, that everyday acts take on a meaning and a life of their own. Even the most ordinary gestures of everyday life hold the possibility of becoming sacred gifts. Gifts that we can give to those fellow travelers we meet somewhere along the road.

Chapter 10

"I'M NOT GRETE."

From the very beginning, this is my motto. It is painted on the shawl that I wear to the race, the one with the fringe of many colors and the big painting of Flash the Miracle Turtle on the back. My friends' big joke, when I first began training, was that I would need some way of letting people know that I was not Grete. I said, "No problem. I'll just paint a big sign on my back saying 'I'm not Grete,' so no one will be confused." They kept the gag going by addressing me as Grete so regularly that customers at my job thought it was my real name.

Even before I knew anything about running, I knew about Grete Waitz. Slender and graceful as a gazelle, she won her first New York City Marathon in 1978, and by 1986 had won eight marathons in nine years, including the last five in a row. She was Norwegian, but there was not a bigger New York star in New York. She owned the marathon. She was the marathon.

In my eyes, it wasn't just her agility or speed or phenomenal record of wins that made her a world-class athlete. She has enormous personal grace and dignity as well: she's the whole package. Seeing her cross the line was enough to give me the chills. Long before I was a marathon fan or even knew why or if the marathon mattered, I was a Grete Waitz fan.

My first marathon is Grete's ninth and final victory, a record that will probably never be broken. That is the first time I experience the sudden descent of helicopters and the rush of motorcycles, cars, and trucks signaling the arrival of the lead runners. We step to the side to cheer the men on; then wait for the next relay of motorcycles and press trucks which will signal the approach of the lead women.

They come not long after the men, and at their head is Grete, running strong and easy and free, her feet barely touching the ground, her stride as effortless as the wind. She is an incredible athlete, and I respect her no end. As she passes, I cheer and applaud. And in my mind, I leash some part of my spirit to her. The next stretch is my miracle mile, the mile that I put in with her. My perfect mile.

She will run in another marathon after that, but she will not win again. That doesn't change the thrill I get when she passes. It doesn't diminish her standing as the very model of grace and competitive fire. And then she retires, and I don't see her again. And as far as I know, I never will.

Then, in 1993, Dick Traum honors Grete and her husband, Jack, at his annual Achilles dinner. He seats me next to her at the head table. All these years I have wanted to meet her, but now that I'm next to her, I am too shy to introduce myself. As you may have guessed, I am not normally shy. Not when it comes to promoting other people's agendas. I'm right up front when I talk to school kids. I don't lack for words when I'm speaking for the MS Society. But when it comes to my own agenda, I'm just not pushy at all.

Grete is shy and reserved as well, and we might have sat there in silence forever had it not been for Dick Traum's taking the initiative and making the introductions. Of course, I don't need an introduction to know who she is. What absolutely floors me is that she knows exactly who I am. She is simply astonished that anyone is willing to stay out on the marathon course for over twenty-four hours. She knows how utterly exhausting two hours and twenty-five minutes can be. To her, an entire day is incomprehensible.

We immediately hit it off at that first meeting, and in no time at all are chatting away, our shyness banished forever. I even have my shawl with me, because I'm supposed to tell a story about it at the dinner, and she thinks it's just great. But it's even better when I tell her the story.

The traditional winner's photo generally carried in the Tuesday morning edition of local newspapers is of the male and female winners wearing their medals and crowns of laurel leaves. The first year I ran, one of the local papers took a picture of me at the finish line and ran it as a small insert under the big picture of Grete in her crown.

The morning after I finish the marathon, I'm on crutches and just barely walking after my twenty-hour adventure. On my way back from the chiropractor, I hail a cab to take me home. It's a standing joke that cab drivers don't speak English anymore, but the driver I get is the classic New York cabby, complete with pasty white complexion and a Brooklyn accent so thick I could have cut it with a chain saw. If I'd sent to central casting for a stereotypical New York driver, this is the guy they'd have sent.

I get in the cab and he looks at me and I can see a light go on in his head. "Hey, I know who you are," he says with a blustery air of certainty. "You were in the paper today. You're that runner. Ya know, the one that won the marathon yesterday. You're Grete What's-Her-Face."

And now, at last, I get to say the words I've been waiting all these years to say: "I'm not Grete." Instead, I tell him, "I'm her older twin sister. People are always mistaking me for her." "Yeah," he says, because New York cabbies are always right. "That makes sense. I knew you looked just like her."

Only in New York could you tell a cabby that you're an older twin sister and get away with it. This is a secret about the city: we like to think of ourselves as the most sophisticated people in the world, but New Yorkers are just as gullible as anyone else.

So now I'm on a roll with this guy. For the rest of the ride, I talk about my twin sister and running marathons and anything else I can make up. And he eats it all up. Somehow, I never get to tell the story at the dinner, but I tell it to Grete, and that's just as good. She thinks it's hilarious.

The dinner is just a few days before my second marathon, and when I tell her that I'm running again, she asks who could possibly be there to record my finish. I tell her that no one is ever there; I call my time in and get a finisher's medal at some point later. That's OK. It's the reality of finishing last, and I certainly don't feel bad about it. Besides, that's not why I run the marathon. It's not for the medal or for a reception at the finish line. It's for me.

She says, "I really think someone should be there." And then she floors me again when she asks if it would be OK if she's that person. "I would be honored," she says. And I think, "Wow!" I mean, here is somebody I have admired forever telling me she wants to be at the finish line when I cross it, and asking if it's all right with me.

I tell her I have no idea when I'll finish, and I wouldn't ask anyone to stand out in the park in the cold for what could be several hours. "It doesn't matter how long it takes you," she says. "I will be there for you when you cross the finish line." I am moved, but I don't allow myself to believe that it will happen. Others have promised before to be there for me, but when the moment came, it just wasn't something they could do. I understand how that works.

This is 1993, the year I do the race with a fibroid tumor the size of a cantaloupe. It has already been biopsied, and I know for sure that it's benign. My doctor and I sit down and talk about it, and she is totally supportive of my waiting to have surgery until after the marathon; it seems a shame to waste a whole year of training. When I ask her what the worst consequence of running could be, she says, "You'll be uncomfortable. *Really* uncomfortable." She is absolutely right. I'm the size of a six-month pregnant woman, and the tumor presses constantly on my bladder and spine. To make things worse, the weather is unseasonably warm and humid, conditions that wipe me out. It takes me twenty-eight hours to finish, so I certainly don't expect the finish line to be any different from the way it's always been.

What I have no way of knowing is that Grete has arranged with Road Runners for the finish line to remain intact until I've crossed it. She is determined that I will experience the race no differently from the almost thirty thousand runners who have crossed the line before me. And the scaffolding remains up, along with the official clock and all the banners.

At six the next morning, she arrives at the line, worried sick that she has already missed me. A friend of mine who is also waiting for me tells her it will be at least another hour before I finish, though he doesn't know for sure. He also tells her that there is no finisher's medal for me.

Grete is incredulous. How can this be? Apparently someone stole a case of medals from the Road Runners headquarters before the race and sold them on street corners, so more than a thousand runners did not get medals at the end of the race. Instead, they were promised that medals would be mailed to their homes.

"She has to have a medal," Grete says. Then she gets an idea. The previous day, her husband, Jack, had run the race as a recreational runner. She asks whether there is enough time for her to run back to her hotel, a mile or so away, and get her husband's medal. More than likely, my friend says.

The greatest female runner ever sprints out of the park and runs up to her hotel room. She barges in the door and wakes Jack. "I need your medal!"

Groggy, he asks what's going on. "Don't worry," she says. "I know someone who needs it more than you do. If you have to have a medal, you can have one of mine." With that, she sprints back to the finish line. In addition to the medal, she brings something else—a bouquet of roses.

Every woman who finishes the marathon gets a single red rose along with her medal. I have never gotten the rose either. Grete is determined that this year I will.

I am still hours away, but she stays at the line, waiting patiently for my arrival. At last I make the final turn into the park, salute the twenty-six-mile marker, and begin the last 385 yards. The first thing I see is that the finish line has been left up for me. As I draw closer, I see that two people are holding a tape across the line, the same tape the winners ran through almost a full day earlier. And then I see the person waiting behind the tape—Grete Waitz. Other people are holding an American flag and a Norwegian flag.

As I cross, she drapes the medal around my neck and we collapse into each other's arms, sobbing with the emotion of the moment. She tells me how much she respects what I've done, and I thank her with every atom of my being for being there for me.

She will be there every year after that, always making sure that the cameras don't get too close, that I have a chair to sit on, that I get water, and that I am warm enough.

We keep in touch throughout the year. And when we get together, we talk about the things that runners everywhere talk about. Best times, worst times, protein drinks, training, cross training, hideous races, bad weather, good weather, and so on. I can't put in a hundred miles a week, as she often does, but we find that many of our training routines are similar.

And I come to realize that there are more similarities between us than differences. This is the gift that Grete and the other elite runners have given me—the knowledge that I am part of the tribe, that I am not an outcast. The race means the same to us. When we are out on the course, we are on the same adventure, the same quest—we just have different stories to tell at the end. But there is for each of us that crowning moment of achievement at the finish, that glorious moment of payoff for all the training, all the sacrifice, all the blood, sweat, and tears. That moment feels the same whether you go home with the prize money and the car, or you finish where I do or anywhere in between.

Her gift to me, of mentorship and camaraderie, is so important because there is always the element that doesn't feel I should be in the race at all. Every year, there is chatter about instituting a time limit, after which a sweep bus will patrol the course and pick up all the stragglers, whether they want to stop or not. Just about every other major marathon in the world has such time limits. But this is what makes the New York City Marathon such a distinctive and grand race. It is inclusive rather than exclusive. Instead of telling people to get off the course, it urges them to join the adventure.

I continually fear that someday, when I can no longer run, the "serious" runners will have their way, and a time limit will be placed on the marathon. Even if they did that now, it wouldn't harm me as much as it would harm others. I, at least, have had the opportunity to experience the race many times. The people I worry about are those who will come after me. Those who may never have the chance to run at all because anonymous officials have decided they're too slow; and those who may never even consider training for it because they don't want to pursue a goal they have no chance of achieving.

One of the reasons that I and others like me can run the marathon is Fred Lebow. Fred was one of the founders of the New York City Marathon and one of those responsible for building the New York Road Runners Club from a tiny membership to a huge organization that sanctions dozens of runs each year.

Like the masses of people he loved having join his marathon, Fred was an entirely ordinary runner. If anything, he tended to be slow. The reason he could build a great organization like Road Runners is exactly that. He was never an elitist. For him, running was a joy, and he wanted everyone to experience that joy.

In the early 1990s he was diagnosed with brain cancer and, after lengthy treatment and rehabilitation, decided to run the 1992 marathon. He was accompanied every step of the way by his close friend Grete, and of the fifty or sixty marathons he ran in his lifetime, this was by far the most emotional.

All along the route he was hailed and cheered and loved by the hundreds of thousands of spectators. It was the ultimate acknowledgement of his manifold contributions to the sport of running. He and Grete both finished in tears, and the city wept with them. It was a remarkable moment. His finishing time was 5:32:35. It was the last marathon he ever ran.

For many years, rumor had it that I was a major thorn in Fred's paw because of the length of time I was out on the course and my obstinate refusal to run an alternate route. I had no way of knowing for sure, but it made sense to me. Then, in 1993, he waited for me at the finish line of the Road Runners' annual Corporate Challenge race. This is a team event, and hundreds of businesses from all over the metropolitan area get together groups of runners, with the teams competing for best combined time.

The company I work for, Tiger Information Systems, fields a team, and of course I take part in the run. I probably don't have to say we don't win, but we aren't in it for that. It's simply a fun thing to do and a great way for us to bond together outside the workplace. That year, when I finished, Fred was there, and he had tears running down his face.

Fred had already gone through his first round of chemotherapy. He knew his time was limited, and he said he was doing all the things he had meant to do but hadn't gotten around to. One of them was talking to me. "I had to wait and I had to tell you," he said, "how grateful I am to you for bringing grace and class to my marathon all these years. I want you to know that when I think of elite runners, your name is right up there with them. And as long as I have breath in my body, there will always be a place for you in my marathon."

Few words have ever meant as much to me.

I saw more of him after that. He came out to the finish line of the 1993 marathon for me and kidded me, saying, "The only reason you did it in twenty-seven hours is because you cut the course," meaning I'd cheated. I cracked up, but my crew of Guardian Angels, not knowing Fred's sense of humor, got very upset. They thought he was serious, and swore solemnly that they were with me all night and that I'd followed the blue line every inch of the way.

The last time I saw Fred was at another Corporate Challenge the year he died. You know how something in you just turns over and your heart sinks down to your feet? That's how I felt. I knew I would never see him again. I really knew it. Felt it. Tasted it. He was extremely weak, spoke only with difficulty, and was already losing his memory. He mounted a platform to get the race started, but he had someone on each side, supporting him.

I saw him and ran off the course to give him a good-bye kiss and a hug. As I did, he didn't say anything, but his eyes filled with tears, and he managed a weak smile and a nod. So I knew that he recognized me. And he and I both knew we would never see each other again.

Fred Lebow died on October 9, 1994, less than a month before the marathon. A twelve-foot bronze statue of him has been erected near the Tavern on the Green, at Sixty-ninth Street. It overlooks the park and the marathon finish line, a truly proper and fitting memorial.

After Fred passed away, I met one of his sisters, Sarah. She came up to me after I spoke for Achilles at a press conference before the 1996 marathon. I didn't know who she was; had never seen her before. But she introduced herself and said, "My brother asked me to tell you, at the first opportunity I had to meet you, how much he loved you. He really loved you, Zoe. Your name was a household word in our home for all the years he fought cancer."

Sarah and I have kept in touch since then. It's a wonderful parting gift from Fred. It is the gift of friendship.

And it's also the gift of knowing that, as long as I keep showing up from year to year, there has to be a place for me in the marathon. There can't not be. And if there is a place for me, there must be a place for everyone who wants to join the adventure. It is the gift of knowing all of us who put in the hours, who train hard all year round for that one day of glory, are part of the tribe. It is the gift of knowing that we truly belong.

CHAPTER 11

AT FIRST I am flattered. Chase Manhattan, the bank that sponsors the New York City Marathon, has asked me to take part in a program it has begun in conjunction with the city's public school system and the Achilles Track Club. The purpose of the Ambassador Program is to send disabled Achilles athletes into various middle schools to show the students what it's like to be disabled.

This all begins back in 1993. I've been chosen both because I have a good story to tell and because I've already run five consecutive marathons. I have some history. To help introduce the athletes to the students, Chase has made baseball-type trading cards for each of us participating in the program. It's a real kick to see myself in my running gear on the front of the card and to turn it over and see some facts about my running career, with a quote from me: "Have a dream, make a plan. Go for it! You'll get there. I promise." The idea is that, after the program, the kids can get autographs and make a one-on-one connection with each athlete. It's called the Ambassador Program.

But when it's time for me to give my first speech, flattery and excitement turn to terror. I am struck by the realization that, at the tender age of forty-five, I am as old as some of the kids' grandmothers. What can I possibly say to kids who are twelve, thirteen, and fourteen years old? The program lasts an hour, and I can tell them about what it's like to live with MS in a few minutes. After that, what?

The morning of my speech there is one thing I am sure of: the kids are definitely going to get the Technicolor Zoe. I dress well, not only for my personal gratification, but because it's important for them to see that disabled people have a sense of style and color and like to dress up, just like everyone else. I decide to bring along Flash the Miracle Racing Turtle and my shawl of many colors. I also bring my earrings and pins and all the accessories that have become part of my story, part of my history.

Uncertain at first how to proceed, I decide to simply tell them who I am and what the program and the race are about. There is a lectern and a stage, but I don't stand above them and talk at them. I stay down on the floor with them, maneuvering with my crutches so that they can see that I'm not making this up, that I deal with this disability every day of my life. They get to see, up close and personal, that life is a challenge and that I meet the challenge every day. And I let them know that some days I meet it better than others. But I do meet it.

I talk about what the marathon means to me and why I run. I tell them about the significance of Flash, my shawl, and my earrings. It turns out that if you tell people your own truth, from that sacred space where you live and where you dream, then age becomes irrelevant. It doesn't matter whether your audience is twelve or eighty. They're going to hear you. They're going to understand. They're going to get it.

And I discover that the kids love this. I'm not just another droning adult sent here to bore them into submission. I'm an event, complete with my own props and visual aids.

They find it easy to love me, because they can see I'm having a great deal of fun telling them my stories.

It is an intense and deeply personal experience that far surpasses anything I could have imagined. Each time I talk at a school, the hour flashes by, and I am astounded that I've taken to this like a duck to water. Instead of facing a difficult audience, I find this the perfect venue for my story. As soon as I start, I know that there is potentially much more to the program than simply presenting the predilections of a subculture that these students may or may not be familiar with. It is much larger than "Zoe does the marathon," because, when you come right down to it, that can be a big "so what?" Ultimately, it's about what it takes to be a winner.

WE LIKE TO talk about how easy kids have it these days, but I find that kids don't feel that way at all. And rightly so. I think that being a kid is very, very hard work.

The world of the 1990s is a much larger, far more complex, and infinitely more dangerous place than the world of my youth. In the 1960s, the toughest of the tough carried switchblades, more often than not for the purposes of "show and tell" rather than real-life use. And the really fast kids smoked Marlboros, not crack.

When I was a kid, someone who got into a fight may have come out of it with a black eye and a bloody nose. Absolute worst-case scenario? A split lip, a bump on the head, and a couple of stitches. And the next day there would be endless gossip at school. On the playground, at lunch, and between classes, we would talk of nothing else—taking sides, and apportioning blame. Those of us who were lucky enough to have been there endlessly recounted all the gory details for those of us who were not. But within forty-eight hours the excitement would die down, and we'd turn our collective attention to whatever was next. Sometimes, by the end of the week, the parties involved were on speaking terms again, sometimes not. But in either case, they were alive and still standing to tell the tale.

Now there are guns and someone is dead. No chance for apology. No possibility of reconciliation. Now the psychologists come in and try to patch up the torn psyches and the shattered lives. And sometimes even their most heartfelt efforts are to no avail.

Kids today are forced to make life-altering decisions about drugs, premarital sex, gangs, and violence. Monumental decisions with consequences that can ruin, or even end, a young life are often made between the ages of ten and twelve. Many of the schools I go to are virtual war zones, and casualties are a daily part of life. Every kid I talk to knows someone who has died either from AIDS or random violence. Many have family, friends, or acquaintances who have already done time in prison. For some it is just another casual topic of conversation; for others, it has become a status symbol.

The dwindling resources of our planet are also a major concern for many of the kids I meet. They fear there is just not enough to go around anymore: not enough jobs, not enough opportunities. Most come from spaces of scarcity— scarcity of money, of food, or comfort, of hope. The world they see is divided into haves and have-nots. They know where they fall in that equation, and it's not on the side of plenty. For many of these kids, there is no *child* in childhood. There is just the hood.

The other side of the coin is the overwhelming and unrealistic emphasis on being number one. On having the flashy car, the expensive wristwatch, the obscenely overpriced athletic shoes and team jackets. I assure them that there is nothing wrong with being number one, but it's not something that everyone can be in everything all the time. Does that mean that we fall like chaff by the wayside? I tell them I don't think so.

As I get deeper into the program and as I visit more schools, I put together a program that deals with winning. I do the same thing with kids that I do with adults, because they really are adults, just smaller. I do edit out some of the more adult-oriented stories, but I never water down who I am.

Because so many of the kids I meet are intimately acquainted with death, I tell them about Joseph, who died in my arms on the Sixth Avenue bus. And while they have seen people waste away from drugs, or may have known someone who was shot or knifed, most of them have not witnessed that final moment head on, one to one. But they have seen the process, and they know what it means. The lesson I want to teach is that out of death they can invent life. I believe this can be one of the biggest lessons of their lives—if they will learn it; if I can teach it.

That act of creation, that process of turning death into life, is the essence of what it means to win. They need to understand this because they don't see themselves as winners, don't see themselves as number one. For many of them, the guy dealing drugs on the corner is number one, or the guy with the Benz, or the guy with the 9 mm Glock. They are all too often people who, from a distance, seem to be winners. A kid looks at them and the money they make, and figures why take a minimum-wage job at a fast-food restaurant when you can make an easy hundred dollars a day dealing crack.

Or they define winning by owning Air Jordan shoes or a Dallas Cowboys jacket, or heavy-duty fourteen-carat-gold jewelry. They see they can get that by taking a job as a stock clerk right now and forgetting about high school. Because they don't see themselves as going beyond high school, don't envision themselves as having anything better than what they see around them.

I tell them about the TV-set theory of life and how the channel they're watching isn't the only one on the dial. There are hundreds and thousands of channels, but they have to be willing to choose and change the channel. And that doesn't mean just *trying* to change it. There is a universe of difference between trying and doing.

Sometimes—maybe all the time—it's complicated, not as easy as pointing the remote control at the set and pushing a button. They have to get off the couch, off their tails, and go push the buttons, fiddle with the connections, fix the horizontal and vertical holds, adjust the contrast, and balance the colors.

Many take off with the TV metaphor. It's a very real image to them because so much of their time and energy are wrapped up with the media, with the images and stories that flash and flicker in front of them.

I find my disability to be an advantage, because kids know even better than adults that we are all disabled in some way. Right now, they feel as if they don't fit in their bodies, which are awash with a riot of hormones and awkward emotions. In one way or another they all feel disabled: not pretty enough, not smart enough, not talented enough, not good enough . . . the list goes on forever. So when I tell them they can't sit there waiting to be cured—waiting for the channel to change—they believe me. They can see that, despite our difference in age, I am where they are—every day of my life.

And disability can be a great teacher. I don't know whether I would have learned everything I have without MS. I might have learned it in other places or other ways, but I can't deny that MS has taught me a great deal. Patience. Humor. Discipline. Humility.

The kids are also impressed when I tell them I didn't run my first marathon until I was forty. They see that it is never too late to reinvent themselves, that they are not too old to change. As young as they are, some of them see life passing them by. They don't see a way out, and therefore they have no stake in the present. If there is no future, why bother being conscious of the here and now? For many kids, that's where the drugs come in. Drugs provide the unconsciousness they seek.

I try to show them the great truth in the old proverb "Where there's a will, there's a way." An important part of that "way" is the ability to set fixed goals. Most people don't have those kinds of goals. They can't see an outcome, can't envision the end result. Maybe they have a goal, but they define it in wishy-washy terms. "Gee, wouldn't it be nice if I . . ." Whatever. You sink into that mode, and you'll never get it done. Instead of inventing reality, reality will invent you. I've learned that life is hard and then you don't die. You probably get to hang around for another fifty or sixty years. And what you do with that time is up to you.

I tell them to set a specific goal and build a plan that will get them there. And whatever the goal is, it has to be worthy of them. It has to demand a lot of their attention and time. It really has to matter to them. They have to know what it will look like when they get there. What they will feel inside. What they will hear and see and touch. Kids are good at imagining and constructing. They know how to do it. They're not ready to give up as long as someone can help show them the way to something better.

Once they set a goal, they have to enjoy the process of getting there. For some reason, we forget it is important to love the process from moment to moment, so we spend a lot of time saying, "Let's get this over with." We want fast food, fast modems, fast baseball games, fast everything. And pretty soon we *do* get it over with—and we are Joseph on the floor of the bus.

OVER THE YEARS, the program has evolved. In 1996, I went into the school system with Grete Weitz and Bill Rodgers, two of the all-time greatest champions in the world of running. That added the important element of letting the kids see both ends of the spectrum of winning. Here are the champions who go home with the cars, the contracts, and the product endorsements. They talk to the kids about the commitment, discipline, and consistency it takes to make it to the top, and they share their personal stories of triumph and defeat. They reinforce the all-important idea that winning is ultimately about doing your personal best, and accepting the outcome of that best with dignity and grace.

And then, of course, at the other end of the race, there are people like me, who don't get all the material prizes but have the same deep satisfaction of achieving something of great personal significance.

By the end of our presentation, the kids can see that winning exists on a far broader continuum than most of them have ever suspected. And even those who were at first resistant are able to see the unlimited possibilities inherent in the word *win*. For some, it's a brand-new concept, one they never thought applicable to themselves. They try it on for size. Hesitantly at first, but, as the old adage goes, "A journey of a thousand miles begins with a single step."

Through it all, my goal is to make them see through my eyes, hear through my ears, and feel with my heart. If I can do this, then I've given them the best of what I have to offer. And I know that they, in turn, will be wise enough to take what they need and leave the rest.

In recent years, since the start of my marathon adventures, my friends tell two jokes about me—or at least two that I'm aware of. The first is that I'm the only person they know who is balance-impaired enough to attempt suicide by leaping off a curb, and the second is that there are eight million stories in the Naked City and at this stage of the game at least half of them are mine. Both are quite true.

I would have to say that at least half of those eight million stories come from school kids. Enough to fill a volume or two. Some are amazing, some are poignant, and some are just downright funny. Since there obviously isn't the time or space to tell them all, I'm going to go with the one that comes to mind right off the bat.

It all started with Diana Townsend, an English teacher from JHS 56 on Henry Street in New York City. She spotted a newspaper article about my marathon and read it to her class. The kids were intrigued. What kind of a person would spend more than a full day out on the marathon course? What did it all mean? And if I went to other schools, why couldn't I come to theirs? They decided to start a letter-writing campaign, telling me what they thought about my marathon and inviting me to their school. I accepted that first year and have done so every year since. It has become a much anticipated reunion on my calendar of special events.

He was twelve the first time I went to JHS 56. Smart. Funny. Endearing. A walking encyclopedia of Elvis trivia and Golden Oldies lyrics. He was one of my all-time favorite kids. During the year, I'd run into him several times in my neighborhood while waiting for a bus. It was always a pleasure to spend a couple of minutes catching up with his life. And then for about a year, our paths didn't cross at all.

The next time I saw him was at his school. I hardly recognized him. He had done the thing that adolescents have a way of doing so well—he'd grown up overnight. He was a full foot taller, thirty pounds lighter and had the beginnings of facial hair to boot.

Much to my surprise, he asked me out. To a Golden Oldies concert, of course. I thanked him for the invitation. While looking for an appropriate response, it dawned on me that maybe he'd forgotten how old I actually was. I inquired after his family, his mother in particular, whom I'd briefly met and spoken to over the phone. Really nice lady.

"She's great," he said. "She'll be glad to know I got a chance to see you again."

"You know," I said, as if it had just occurred to me, "your mom is about my age." I figured this would be the ultimate reality check. Most kids are really grossed out by the thought of hanging out with someone from their parents' generation.

"Oh, God, no!" he responded, genuinely shocked. "You're *much* older than my mother. I mean *way, way* older." Then, with a resigned sigh, he said, "Listen, the way I look at it is like this. I don't really care how old you are. Years don't matter. 'Cause deep down inside, you have the heart of a twenty-year-old. So . . . I'm fourteen, you're twenty. Six years. That's do-able."

I declined his gracious offer as tactfully as possible. He's moved on to senior high school now and will no longer catch up to me in the hall on my yearly visits to his school. I'll miss him. My life was always a better place for having seen the world through his eyes—if only for five minutes. His teachers shake their heads and chuckle when they think of him. They miss him too.

He's the kind of kid you'll remember twenty years from now when you need a reason to smile. And you'll silently send him a blessing, hoping all the while that the reality of his life has at least matched and perhaps exceeded his potential.

During my visits kids always ask who my own heroes and heroines are. I say they're the everyday people I meet along the way in life. People who lead their lives with integrity, purpose, compassion, and humor. And since I've been involved in the Ambassador Program, teachers are high on my list.

The way I look at it is that I come into their schools once a year and speak for an hour. For them, I am an hour off from regular classes, an event. But the teachers keep coming back every day. They are the process. They come from a space of integrity and commitment, and every day, year in and year out, they have to deal with the politics of the New York public school system. In many schools the teachers spend their own money for supplies; otherwise the kids wouldn't have what they need to learn properly.

So I tell the kids they should appreciate their teachers a little more, that the level of commitment and consistency they're bringing to their jobs is both astounding and outstanding. They are my heroes and heroines now.

To tell the truth, I didn't really have many heroines as a kid. I liked Nancy Drew in the mystery book series because she kicked some serious butt and she never backed down or gave up. She was one tough cookie. You could tie her up, lock her in the attic, or poison her, and it didn't matter. She'd keep coming back for more. And one way or another, no clue went unnoticed and no mystery remained unsolved.

Of all the fictional heroines in the literature of my youth, the one that disappointed and let me down the most is Louisa May Alcott's Beth in *Little Women*. I loved Beth when I read the book as a kid. And then she got sick and died. Just like that. Good old Louisa May just killed her off in two or three flowery sentences about the birds singing and the flowers blooming, and Beth dying. That outraged me. Maybe because I was afraid of giving up before my time, of not fighting the good fight. Maybe I was afraid of becoming her. And maybe, somewhere in a dark and secret corner of my heart, that childhood fear remains.

Anyway, I've been careful about picking heroes and heroines ever since. And, given the state of the world, that's probably a good thing.

I take it very seriously, though, when any of the kids I

talk to adopts me as a role model. A lot of athletes today insist they are not role models. They think that's a job for parents. But sometimes you don't have the choice. When you become a public figure, even to the limited extent that I have, people are going to watch how you behave. I believe I have an obligation to be a positive example. If you care about the future of the planet, there's really no choice involved.

And you never know when it will come back to you. Three years after I first started doing the Chase program, we were plugging along in the marathon through one of the worst neighborhoods in Brooklyn when a gang of kids ran out to meet me. One of their friends had seen me at his school the first year of the program and had gotten a baseball trading card with my picture on it. He kept the card, took it home, and told his friends about the woman with the turtle and the shawl who does the marathon.

The story he told them was actually much better than the one I had told him. It sounded as if I were in the middle of Armageddon and had to karate-chop my way through bands of evildoers and wild animals. I didn't mind the embellishment, since the fundamental points about winning remained intact.

Anyway, these kids who ran out to see me—Aaron, Jovonne, and Joi—had never heard me speak. But they told me my story as if each word had been spoken to them directly. Their mother, Johan, told me later that they were completely intractable on marathon Sunday. They didn't want to do any chores, because they were afraid that they would miss me when we came by. They took a vote, and Joi, the youngest, sat by the window all afternoon on Zoe

Watch. When I finally came into view, she and her brother and sister came running out of the house at full speed. No coats or hats or gloves in sight.

Then their mother came charging out behind them, trying to get them to put something on. Only when I promised that we wouldn't leave did they go in and get their coats. We talked for a few minutes, and *they* told me *my* story. Better than I ever could have. If I'm really lucky, maybe I'll get to hear that story again every year. I tend to forget how good a story it really is, and I'm grateful they're there to remind me.

EVERY YEAR, HESTER, the Angels, assorted friends, and I cross the finish line with hundreds of letters written by both kids and adults from all across the country. Many of these gifts of the spirit come from kids who have been in the Achilles Track Club/Chase Manhattan–sponsored school program. I see these letters as a living testament to the success of the Ambassador Program. Kids share their dreams, their fears, and their greatest hopes with me, knowing that their letters will cross the finish line with us. It makes them part of the journey. It makes them part of the adventure. It enables us to bring to full cycle the relationship begun in the classroom or auditorium. It enables us to cross the finish line together.

CHAPTER 12

IT IS CLOSING in on two A.M. Twenty hours on the road. Almost seven miles and eight hours to go. And the guy on the radio is saying, "This is a joke. The Angels should be out patrolling the subways or busting drug dealers instead of wasting their time with her. Let her do it by herself."

He is saying this to Curtis Sliwa on Curtis's overnight talk show. And he is saying this to me. It is a good thing I am sitting down when he says it, because it's like a punch in the stomach. Especially now, in the dead of night, before we've made the turn for home. Physical and emotional reserves are at an ebb. I am vulnerable. Terribly vulnerable.

We have called a rest stop at 124th Street and First Avenue, just short of the Willis Avenue Bridge, the gateway to the Bronx. As we rest, the Guardian Angels rig me up with a headset and patch me in to Curtis's show on WABC–AM. We do this for a couple of minutes every hour or so through the night. His listeners enjoy keeping tabs on my journey, a real and continuing drama that breaks up the usual overnight fare of people calling up to grouse about politics, social issues, and the sorry state of the universe.

Usually, we talk about where I am on the course, my condition, the weather, the funny, scary, or unusual things that happened in the last hour, people we've met, people who have shown us kindness, that sort of thing. Like the folks who run McDonald's just across the Willis Avenue

Bridge, in the Bronx. Since their opening in 1995, they've opened the restaurant for us when we come by, since it will be hours and miles before we will be able to get a hot drink or the use of an indoor bathroom again. Normally, at that hour, they do only drive-through business. But when we come by, they are just wonderful about it. So we broadcast from there as a validation of their kindness and decency.

Frequently, people call in to say, "Keep going." "You can do it." Or whatever. It's a morale booster for me and good theater for listeners. On occasion, it has been a real lifesaver.

The 1995 marathon is the most brutal ever. It begins in freezing rain and gale winds on the Verrazano Narrows Bridge, and remains cold and raw the rest of the way. That's the year I hit a pothole in the Bronx, crash, and do all kinds of soft-tissue damage. We stagger on through the night, wondering if the sun will ever rise again. They say it's always the darkest just before the dawn. I never really understood that until I started doing marathons. Now I know. It's true.

Curtis saves me that year. It's before sunrise, and we are still hours from the finish line. If you can get any lower than that, I don't want to know about it. The Angels hook me up for my regular update, and I tell Curtis and his audience how rough it is. He says, "Hey, all of you who are on your way to work, bus drivers, sanitation workers, delivery people, honk if you love Zoe."

It is the most amazing thing. All over the city, so eerily quiet in the pre-dawn, we can hear horns honking. It is like a shot of adrenaline. My legs get lighter, as does my spirit. I don't think even today that Curtis fully knows what kind of gift he gave me that year, or what an enormous factor he was in my finishing.

So this is the background and the history against which to set the caller who is now assaulting my very right to exist as an athlete. Just my being on the course infuriates him, and he can't wait to tell me what he's thinking.

"No one," he says, "should be allowed on the course if they can't run the race in like four hours. OK, six hours tops, but that's pushing it." This is a time frame that would eliminate literally thousands of runners. He continues to vent his wrath. "The Angels are wasting their valuable time. They are baby-sitting a real loser. If she really wants to do 26.2 miles, then let her do it on a treadmill some-place, where she's not bothering anybody." I listen to all of this through the headphones. I am speechless.

I've heard talk like this before, yet every word is like a knife plunged into me and then sadistically twisted. I know that not everyone is on my side, and I accept that. Still, the words hurt. And the tears they cause sting.

Hard-edged memories come back. Other times and other places when I heard similar comments. Back when I first started running in shorter races, training for the mara-thon, there were always people eager to tell me to get off the course if that was the best I could do. On a couple of occasions, other runners elbowed me or even tried to knock me down. So I have long known that it doesn't mat-ter if your motivation is good and your heart is pure. You could be doing all the right things for the right reasons, and there are always going to be people who would run you down in the street with their cars if they got half a chance.

I also know the critics are not limited to the able-bodied,

and they come from every angle. I have had people in the disabled community charge me with doing a disservice to disabled athletes, because they feel when people think of disabled athletes they shouldn't be thinking of someone who takes over twenty-four hours to do a race. They should be thinking of disabled athletes who "can really do it."

And there are such people. Many of them. The wheelchair racers who can break two hours and beat the able-bodied runners. The blind runners who break three hours. The amputees, on prosthetic limbs or crutches, who turn in times I can only dream about.

Some people with multiple sclerosis can do the marathon in four hours, a very respectable time. But they're not as balance-impaired as I am. MS is a really funky and bizarre disease. The gamut of symptoms is enormous. Some people have visual problems. Some have occasional bouts of weakness in their limbs that come and go. Some have numbness. Some have facial tics. Still others are in wheelchairs.

And some can run a marathon in four hours, God bless them. That's wonderful, really wonderful. I wish I could too. But I can't, because I have a whole different set of symptoms. I have a whole range of sensory problems that are admittedly low grade as MS goes, but they are constant. I'm on crutches for my own safety.

For these people, then, my sin isn't being disabled. If I were a whiz, that would be no problem at all. What they can't forgive me for is being slow. I can't help that. I'd be delighted to finish in the middle of the pack or to finish in four hours. I can't. If I finish in twenty-eight hours, that's my rock-bottom best. So having people sneer and say, "Is that the best you can do?" is a hurtful blow. Because the answer is yes. And let me tell you something. Eight months of the year, I spend more time with Richard Simmons and his "Sweatin to the Oldies" tapes than I do with my family and friends. There are hours and hours of training on the road, in the gym, doing aerobic tapes. And you know what? If I didn't work as hard as I do to get ready, I wouldn't be able to do it in twenty-eight hours. I wouldn't be able to do it at all. If I can live with it, so can you.

And I can honestly say that I've never sought publicity, but it is there, and with each passing year the scene at the finish line has become a little crazier. Being the last runner attracts attention. There are people who blame me for turning the finish line into some kind of media circus and taking the attention away from "real" runners. They don't seem to understand that it has nothing whatsoever to do with me. Reporters seek me out every year. In part, I think it's because from moment to moment I'm really present. I'm about as real as you can get. That's why people come along on the marathon journey and share their lives and their stories with me. I, in turn, carry those stories across the finish line. And what makes them really great is that they're all true. It is that authenticity the reporters cherish and seek out. It's the storytelling, the basic stuff of our humanity. Every year, more stories become part of the journey, and vice versa. Just by showing up every year, I have become part of the city's legend. A city that demands endurance and determination as a prerequisite for life within its confines. Ultimately, my marathons have become a journey that parallels the life of the city.

People don't realize none of it has ever been at my initiation. But if someone puts a microphone in front of me and invites me to speak, I'm going to try to do some good with it. I'll say a few words about the kids' program I do for Chase Manhattan Bank, and I'll talk about the Achilles Track Club, which is very important to me. I'll talk about Marathon Strides, a fundraising program for the MS Society. If that's a circus, so be it. Buy me a black top hat and a riding crop and call me ringmaster. Or ringmistress, as the case may be.

We say in the United States that we are about freedom and pursuing our dreams, but there are always people who think we should pursue only dreams they approve of. I have found over the years that disapproval can come from everywhere and anywhere. And sometimes from the most shocking and least anticipated of sources.

For instance, there is a radio station in New York with a regular program devoted to the disabled and the issues that affect them. One day, I was invited to be a guest on a show dealing with disabled celebrities. The Miss America at the time, who was deaf, was on during one segment before me.

Between Miss America and me was a segment called "Having My Say." The person doing that segment, via telephone, was the editor of a militant newspaper for the disabled. She started out by saying that her newspaper never does articles on the celebrity disabled, because she believes that such people inflict a great deal of harm on the entire disabled community. She was not allowed to name names or point a finger at anyone specifically, but it was clear she was talking about me. I was the next guest, and she knew it.

She called me a "super gimp" and said that people like me made it impossible for "normal disabled" people to have a life. In the job market, she said, when businesses look to hire the disabled, they expect a super gimp because of what they've seen on television or in the newspapers. They get the impression that there are only two kinds of disabled: super gimps and totally useless life forms.

Her point was that disabled people are normal people, just like everyone else. And people like me, who run two-day marathons or bungee-jump in wheelchairs, do so "out of a neurotic inability to accept our limitations."

Those were heavy words. Fighting words.

She said the unfortunate thing was that disabled kids look to super gimps as role models, and that was only setting them up for disappointment. When the host, Bob Enteen, asked her who she thought should be role models for the disabled community she said, "Oh, disabled teachers, disabled business people, disabled congresspeople."

I wanted to scream, "Are you crazy? You've got to be a real super gimp to get to Congress! That's a job that not many able-bodied people aspire to. You've got to be kidding me!" I couldn't believe her flawed logic or that she was making judgments about me, when she has no idea who I am, what I do, or what I use my celebrity for.

But I couldn't talk. This was a monologue, one person's opinion, and I was not allowed to break in. For once in my life, it was a good thing I couldn't speak, because I have no idea what would have come out of my mouth. I was flabbergasted at the very thought that someone could actually feel that way. To be called a super gimp, with the words uttered as a vile expletive, and to be told that people are disgusted by my marathon adventures and dismissive of all the work I do in schools and for charity, was nothing short of decimating. It would have been intolerable enough to be considered a super gimp by an able-bodied person. But to be told this by someone in my own subculture was inconceivable.

So I sat in stunned silence, smoldering at her absurd view of the disabled world. Because what she was complaining about are the same things that apply to normal people. Should Michael Jordan quit playing basketball because kids will be disappointed when they learn they can't do what he does? Do we quit telling kids, "You can grow up to be President," because it's unrealistic?

I thought she was missing the whole point. What we really need is to reinvent the word *win* so that it encompasses the small daily triumphs we experience every day of our lives. We don't necessarily need to kick out the top players. Just make the playing field bigger. Make the team global.

There was a break after she had had her say and before I went on. Bob asked me if I wanted to respond to her, without addressing her personally and starting a war. I said, "After sitting and listening to her for five minutes, I still don't know what she wants. I have no clue. No clue at all."

What does she want me to do? Lie down and die? Would that suit her? Does that fit her definition of appropriate limitations? When I find out what my boundaries are, I'll be the first to know. Then I'll write her a letter so she can be the second. But with any kind of luck, I'll never know what my boundaries are because I'll always be busy inventing new ones. If that makes me a super gimp, so be it. Then that's who I am. Super Gimp Ringmistress.

I mean, here is someone who is disabled herself, and yet puts out a newspaper, accusing me of being a super gimp. I may well feel just as inadequate because I can't put out a newspaper, too. Where does it stop?

Finally, I told Bob, "I wouldn't even know how to respond." So I talked about being a "celebrity disabled" person and ignored her speech. I let my story speak for itself. And I decided that I will never stop testing my boundaries, because, ultimately, that's what it's all about: testing boundaries. Too many of us never find out what our boundaries are. We allow ourselves to be confined in cages that have no bars or walls, prisons of our own making. And then we get angry when someone challenges our assumptions.

This is what the editor of the disabled newspaper did. What she did to me in the light of day the caller to Curtis's program is doing in the dead of night. But instead of calling me a super gimp, he is calling me a total loser.

Curtis tells him that he is wrong, that I am an athlete. But the caller, whose idea of action is sitting home on his couch and telling other people how to run their lives, cannot wrap his mind around the image of anyone like me as an athlete. In his universe, athletes are the people who win the races, not the ones who come limping in behind. People like me simply don't matter.

"Let him come out on the course," I say. "Let him catch up to us and see how and if it matters."

Another Achilles athlete, listening at home, calls the station and challenges the man to come to one of our workouts and try to keep up with some of us. Needless to say, our anonymous critic did not rise to the occasion.

I maintain my poise on the air, but when I take the headset off, I am deeply wounded. We are in those darkest hours of the night, long before life will return to the city. Something like this can be devastating if you give it power. But I realize that this guy is essentially a nobody, a disembodied voice in the darkness, ultimately of no consequence in my life. He probably has no life of his own, devoting his insomniac hours to venting his spleen on a captive radio audience. Everywhere he looks he sees losers, but the biggest loser of all is the loser inside his soul.

But even though it's old and it's tired, it won't go away. There are always people who feel as he does. A lot of them are too polite or too politically correct to say so, but you can see it in their eyes, feel it in their handshake. If you have any empathy at all, you'll know. You'll know.

Tears fill my eyes and run down my cheeks as I look up at the Angels. They are a tough breed who hold their emotions in check, and they don't know what to do, so they do that guy thing, where they shuffle around and look at the ground. They're caught between wanting to touch me to make it better and being afraid that might make it worse. I can see they are mad and feeling their own hurt at what has happened. They are supposed to protect me, but they have been powerless against this voice coming over the airwaves, questioning my very existence and theirs as well.

Finally, one of the Angels says, "You are one of us. You have the warrior spirit."

In my heart, I know he's right. Maybe what happened is actually a good thing. It's a test and an opportunity for all of us to rally together and draw strength from one another.

The man called me a baby and said the Angels are babysitting me. That line comes back to me as I grab my crutches, hoist myself to my feet, and get ready to move out again.

"I don't know about you guys," I tell the Angels, "but this baby has a bridge to run."

CHAPTER 13

IT IS 1995: not the Marathon from Hell, but the Marathon through Hell. In case you ever doubted it, trust me: Hell freezes over. And believe me, you don't want to be there when it does.

Every year until now, this has been our special time, six A.M., when Hester and I take our first steps onto the Verrazano Bridge and into a new dawn, a new adventure.

But today there is no dawn. There is wind howling like a legion of banshees. There is cold, biting and clawing at our skin. There is icy rain, driven horizontally by the wind. And there is darkness, alive and malevolent, filled with foreboding, as black as Armageddon. The bridge does not stretch ahead, inviting and wonderful. It disappears into the blackness, its mighty towers swallowed up by clouds and rain and darkness. It is a bad day for a marathon.

But it is the only day we have, and when the starter says go, Hester and I go. We do not go dancing and singing "Follow the Yellow Brick Road," but hunched over, with gritted teeth. Hester is anchored by the luggage trolley she pulls bearing the two knapsacks that carry our supplies. Adding just the right surrealistic touch is a film crew from Japan that will follow our every step.

Normally, this is the time we drink in the approaching dawn, and celebrate not only our own journey, but the journeys of all the thousands who will themselves cross the bridge hours from now. It is the time we pause at the crest of the bridge, drinking in the view that seems to go on forever. But today there is no view, no joy—simply survival. Step by treacherous step.

Then, just when we think it can't possibly get more miserable, it does. The stinging rain turns to icy pellets of snow. Hester and I both notice the change in precipitation at the same time. It's a pivotal moment when we both could have burst into tears. Instead, we give each other that silent look that says, "What's next?" and burst into gales of laughter. Snow on the Verrazano Bridge on marathon morning? Who'd have "thunk" it? The wind is so intense, it's hurts to laugh. As a matter of fact, it hurts just to breathe, but we really can't help ourselves. The absurdity of our situation overwhelms us. Where is that Achilles coach, with her dire warnings about laughter and oxygen deficit on the bridge, when we really need her?

The laughter is instinctive, our special defense against the forces of nature. Throughout the years and the miles, we have always laughed. We laughed at the rats after we fled their charge in Central Park. We laughed when I crashed in the Bronx and dragged a half-dozen people down on top of me. It is the same instinct that tells me I cannot accept this start as the seedling from which our day will grow.

I know that we must let go of this negativity, refuse to give it the power that, by tradition, goes to the dawn and the bridge. Otherwise, I'll create a horrible day for myself, because if I see this beginning on the bridge as my siren song, that song is going to be a funeral dirge before the day is done. No way am I going to allow that to happen.

The bridge is a mile across, and normally that's a half-hour's journey. Today, it takes more than an hour, with each step a gasping, staggering battle. I am wearing every layer of clothing I have with me, but none of it is of any use. Hester has a layer in reserve somewhere in the bottom of her backpack. I can't wear the plastic thigh-length poncho that comes with the marathon entrant's kit, just as I cannot wear nonporous waterproof garments of any kind. As they keep the water out, they also keep body heat in, and once I'm overheated, I do not cool down. A very common quandary faced by many people with MS.

So the rain and snow and sleet hit and stick and soak through to my skin and then to my bones. The only parts of me that are dry are my feet, because I have at least thought to wear boots. They are ugly, horrible, size-twelve men's galoshes, the only things I could find to fit over my sneakers. They are not easy to walk in, but at least they keep the rain out.

We've been doing this for seven years and figure we've seen everything. We've done hot and cold. We've done rain and shine. But snow has never before entered the equation. It has never entered the Road Runners marathon equation either. After we set out, they close the bridge entirely. Many wheelchair athletes, unable to keep warm in the staging area, never start at all. Because of the potential dangers presented by the high wind velocity, other Achilles runners are bused over the bridge and given an alternative start. But since no one knew what it would be like when we set out, we go the usual route.

When we finally get back down to land in Bay Ridge, Brooklyn, I turn around and face the bridge. I do this every year, and when I do, I put my hands together as if in prayer and bow reverentially to my friend the bridge. That final view to me is not only a symbol of where we've been, but a promise of where we have yet to go. This day when I turn around, a final blast of howling wind hits me and all but knocks me on my keester. When it does, I look at Hester and say something that, when cleaned up for family consumption, translates to "Screw this garbage." We are drenched and miserable, but when I say that, Hester cracks up, and I with her. For the rest of that marathon, whenever Hester needs something to laugh about—and we'll face that need more often than ever before or since—she hauls out that line and we laugh again.

Now that the bridge is behind us for another year, we try to figure out what to do. For seven years, my constant fear has been that of overheating. It never dawned on me that I could also go into hypothermia. Right now, that is beyond a mere possibility; it's a distinct reality. We are shaking from head to foot, and our teeth are chattering around in our heads. The wind isn't as awful as it was on the bridge, with nothing to stop it, but the damage has been done. Our clothing is plastered to our bodies, and the wet fabric is wicking the heat out of us at a frightening rate.

We have no idea how far we can go like this and no clue as to what to do. The rain and snow have let up, and we wonder whether the wind will dry our clothing before we freeze, or will simply freeze our clothes, encasing us in ice. This is so beyond the realm of normal experience, we are at a complete loss.

As we shiver and debate our options, we approach a bar. We are on Fort Hamilton Parkway in Bay Ridge, and the bar's name is Thirstees. It is closed after what was probably a long and boisterous night. The only person around is the porter, a short, balding man with glasses, a man who looks as if he's lived hard, working through the darkest hours of the night and into the early morning, cleaning up the place. He is sweeping the night's debris from in front of the bar into the gutter, where the wind and rain run-off conveniently take it away. When he looks up from his sweeping, there we are: two women, one on crutches and the other dragging a luggage cart laden with knapsacks and covered with plastic garbage bags. Our bulky, layered clothing is soaking wet and our hair is covered with icicles.

He looks at us as if we've just stepped off a spaceship. For all he knows, that's exactly what we've done. Either that, or we're a couple of homeless women who somehow got lost over here at the tail end of Brooklyn. In any event, our teeth are literally chattering and we present a pretty scary sight. On top of that is the matter of the film crew, which is also something that can make real New Yorkers wary.

As he looks us over, we can see his mental wheels turning. He is a classic Brooklynite, and as a New York lifer myself, I know what he's thinking. He's alone in the bar, and his job is to clean the place up, not to play Good Samaritan.

We say, "Hi," and tell him we're the first runners and we've just come over the bridge and we're pretty much frozen. In Iowa, this probably plays immediately. But this is Brooklyn, and he's no doubt heard better stories. Then I unzip my jacket and he sees my marathon number. At that point he knows we're for real, and his reserve melts in an instant.

"Come on," he says, solicitous now. "Come on inside."

"Are you sure it's OK?" we ask.

"Sure," he says. "Anyway, I can't leave you to freeze in

front of my door. Then I'd have to sweep you up too, more work than I'm willing to do at this hour of the morning."

We introduce ourselves to him and he to us. His name is Artie. He ushers us in, and now I have another adjustment to make, the reintroduction of heat into my existence. "Go sit on the radiator," Artie says. "In another ten minutes the laundromat across the street will be open and you can dry your things there."

You can almost see the light bulbs turn on over our heads. Of course! This is a residential neighborhood, and if your clothes are wet, you find a laundromat and dry them out. That's what you do in real life: more of what works and less of what doesn't. It's something so obvious that we want to slap ourselves upside the head for not thinking of it right off the bat.

As we sit and wait, toasting our buns on the radiator, Artie gets us orange juice and regales us with stories about the bar and his job. He has the normal gift of gab of a man who usually spends a lot of time listening to and trading stories. He has a keen sense of what makes a good story, and immediately sees the potential in this one. But to tell it properly, he'll need all the juicy details, so he interviews us with the skill of a veteran tabloid journalist. He asks what we're doing out so early. We explain about my MS and about how long it takes me to finish. There's a possibility, I tell him, that I may be the last finisher.

"So let me get this straight," Artie says. "When you finish, it will have been because I let you in here to warm up, right?"

"Right," I tell him. "And if anyone asks, tell them you saved the lives of Zoe and Hester. And because you did what you did, we'll do what we do."

The camera crew isn't having nearly as much fun as we are. They had no idea what they were getting into or what it takes for me to get through the day. And they can't understand what's holding me up. They don't realize that if I go out with wet clothing, I'm dooming myself to losing control of my race—and of not finishing at all.

They're thinking of the finish line, and I can't afford to think that far ahead. Not now. Not yet. I'm still at the start, and I have to turn this day around and point it in a direction that works. And the way to do that is to wait till the laundromat opens and dry my clothes.

Finally, the laundromat opens. We thank Artie, and he exacts a promise from us to give him credit for saving our lives if we get a chance to do any media interviews. Hugs and handshakes all around as we bid him a fond farewell.

Safely across the street and indoors again, we face a new problem. Hester still has a change of clothing, but I am wearing all the clothes I brought with me, and they're all soaking wet. What do I wear while they're drying?

The answer is obvious, although not the one I like. I pull on my little marathon rain poncho and struggle out of my wet clingy clothes underneath it, trying not to attract too much attention: a major contradiction in terms. I then proceed to sit in my underpants with the poncho covering little more than a hospital gown would. I've got to tell you honestly, if a magic genie had come down and offered to grant me one solitary wish, would I have wished for world peace or an end to global hunger? Hell, no, I'd have wished for a faster dryer.

Fortunately, the laundromat is big enough so that we can sort of hide in the back, out of sight of the woman who runs the place from a booth in the front. And since it's early, there are very few other customers, and they are in front by the washing machines. They notice us, but they're nice enough not to stare or ask questions. Or maybe, with this being New York, they figure we're crazy and, if they just ignore us, eventually we'll go away.

As the dryer does its thing, I'm thinking that this does not fit my picture of what marathon morning is supposed to look like. My internal cycle of self-reproach is in full gear: I should have done this; I could have done that; I'm losing precious time; I'm already an hour behind pace . . .

Finally, I tell myself to just shut up. OK, so I didn't know. Well, now I do. And I can either have my whole day and my whole race be about this, or I can stop beating myself up and get on with it. Right now I'm in a laundromat. My clothing is almost dry. The dragon is slain. So I took some casualties in this one battle; there's a whole war to be waged yet. The elements may not improve, but, if we need them, there are a hundred laundromats along the route. And if that's what I have to do to get done, that's what I'll do. And I'll keep on doing it until I get to the finish line.

I remember one year when Grete Waitz had an intestinal bug, she had a choice of leaving the course to hit a portable john every couple of miles, thereby losing the race, or figuring out a way to keep running. So she got a pack of tissues and kept on running, cleaning up after herself as she went along. And all the while, the cameras followed her, recording every detail. Now Grete is a woman of enormous dignity, but she is also a champion athlete, and she understood that what was important was the outcome, not how she looked along the way. In spite of everything, she won the race. Hands down. No contest.

For me, it's back to the television set again. If the program that's on doesn't fit my picture, then I need to change the channel. For a short while, I had been on the Drama Queen Network and—I must admit—loving every minute of it. But now I change to the Comedy Channel. It finally dawns on me that this is very, very funny and that Artie isn't the only one who will have a preposterous story to tell.

I mean, here I am on marathon Sunday, sitting in my underpants in a Korean laundromat in Bay Ridge, Brooklyn, waiting for my clothes to dry. You just can't make this stuff up. If I tried, I couldn't think of anything more absurd. You could have asked me at any given moment before the marathon where I'd be a seven A.M. on Sunday, and I never would have come up with my present reality. Not in a million years! No way would I be sitting in my underwear. I'd be filled with derring-do and performing great deeds, maybe singing a song, maybe looking forward to that first cup of hot tea. But I'm not. So get off it. Get over it. And get on with it.

When the dryer finally stops, there is a definite upside, although it's not trying to get dressed under a tiny poncho while being spastic. It's the feeling of toasty, old-time comfort and joy when I finally climb into my warm long johns and the rest of my clothing, and Hester and I get back on the road.

The pounding rain has stopped, and it only drizzles on and off for the rest of the way. That's a blessing, but it remains windy and bitterly cold. As night approaches and we get ready to hook up with the Guardian Angels, I call ahead and remind them to bring plenty of extra clothing. Macho doesn't cut it in forty-five-mile-an-hour winds. You've got to have warm, dry clothing.

It becomes the longest marathon ever for me—twenty-nine hours and fifteen minutes. In the middle of the night, Grete, who'd promised again to meet me at the finish line, wakes up in her hotel, hears the wind howling, and wakes her husband, Jack. "What is it?" he asks.

"It's Zoe," she says. "I'm worried that she's out there in this kind of weather. What will happen to her?"

"You know her well enough to know she'll be fine," he reassures her. "She may not finish early, but she'll finish."

And I do. With a wrenched elbow, bruised legs, two nails torn off at the quick, and assorted scrapes and bruises all over my body. I look as if I've been in a boxing match, not a marathon. All courtesy of a nasty fall into a Bronx pothole. I finish cold, exhausted, and, needless to say, elated.

There are some reporters at the finish line and I do tell them about Artie, but he doesn't make their stories. The following year, we stop again at Thirstees, just to say thank you. Again Artie is outside, sweeping the butt ends of another Bay Ridge Saturday night into the gutter. Again we say, "Hi!"

At first he ignores us; then he snorts at us. He's ticked off, he says. He saw me on TV last year and I didn't mention him. Didn't mention him at all. I tell him that I did, but it didn't get past the editors. He says that's a likely story.

He's not really all that ticked off, though, and finally he gives in and welcomes us to use the bathroom and chug down a fast glass of orange juice. And this time we don't have to get dry, and I don't have to fight my way through to a different channel.

Once again, I promise Artie I'll mention him if there's any kind of media coverage. Much to my surprise and delight, I end up appearing on the *Rosie O'Donnell Show* that year. And at last his kindness becomes a matter of public record.

I also promise him that if I ever write a book about my marathon adventures, he'll be a prominent part of it. Maybe even have his own chapter. I'm a woman of my word. And so, Artie, this is just for you.

You're part of our legend now, and we're part of yours. If you hadn't taken us in that horrible morning back in 1995, we might never have found the laundromat, might not have even thought of it ourselves until it was too late. And maybe we never would have finished. So now you're not just part of the legend, but part of the reality. You're a regular stop now. A clean bathroom break, a glass of juice, and five minutes of lively conversation. What could get those twelve miles in Brooklyn off to a better start?

But more than that you're a source that I can draw on in the middle of the night when I need to remember the goodness of New Yorkers and the kindness of one in particular, something to keep me going. You're a constant reminder that you do what you gotta do in life to get where you wanna go—and often it's not going to fit your preconceived picture.

Thanks for the life lesson, Artie. See you next year. Same time. Same place.

CHAPTER 14

HER NAME IS Shari Fogler, and she never knew her grandmother. Shari knew of her, though, of her lust for life, her strength of spirit, her courage. And Shari knew of her grandmother's blue eyes, a blue as clear and pure as a flawless sky. No one in the family has ever seen eyes like that again.

Shari's grandmother died young, the victim of a chronic progressive form of multiple sclerosis. Although the disease killed her, she remained undefeated. Right up to the end, she never stopped being fully alive.

These were the stories Shari heard while growing up, wonderful stories about a wonderful woman. And even though Shari never met her, she was left with a sense of loss, a feeling of being incomplete.

So now it is the autumn of 1994, time for another New York City Marathon. This will be for me the year that the NBC *Today Show* wires me for sound and sends a camera crew and a truck to follow me for all but the last couple of miles of the race. When a producer first contacted me, I was reluctant to agree to the idea. It's a big risk to lay yourself out there with every word and move being recorded. Things can get pretty personal at times. But the more I talked to him, the more convinced I became that he and I had the same view of the marathon. He understood that it is a personal journey that parallels the life of the city—a day in the life.

The piece they put together is extraordinary. It runs for twelve minutes, an eternity by television standards. Katie Couric and Bryant Gumbel interview me live from the course about a mile from the finish line. And as they are wrapping up the show, just before ten A.M., they show me crossing the finish line.

Shari sees the program, and it strikes a hundred nerves. All the incomplete business about her grandmother surges to the fore. It is the color of my eyes, the same blue that she thought she'd never see. It is my age, forty-six, the exact age at which Shari's grandmother died. It is the MS, and the journey Shari's grandmother could not complete that I have taken up. It is the life spirit. It is all the things that make up the missing pieces in the puzzle of Shari's family saga.

She becomes determined to contact me, because she wants the personal sense of completion and closure she feels meeting me can give her. But beyond that, Shari is the community resource liaison at Poly Prep, a private school in Brooklyn with a rich history of academic achievement. She feels that if I can take the message she saw on the *Today Show* piece to the student body, it could benefit everyone.

It takes a while, but Shari finally tracks me down and tells me her remarkable story. And I, in turn, tell her stories from the road. Finally she asks whether I would come to her school to address the student body at morning chapel.

Every Monday and Thursday the school day begins with chapel, a twenty- or thirty-minute period when the entire school, grades five through twelve, comes together. The period is an opportunity for the headmaster, Bill Williams, to take care of routine business and to talk about a current event or issue that may be interesting or troubling to the students. I tell Shari I'd be honored to come.

On the appointed day, I find a beautiful campus, alive with tradition. I get the guided tour, and at every turn there is another layer of tradition, pride, and custom. To say the least, I am impressed.

This is a big change for me. Until now, all my speaking engagements at schools have been in New York City's public schools, to kids at the opposite end of the socioeconomic scale. Shari introduces me to the student body and tells her story about her own sense of loss, and why she had spent so much time seeking me out.

It is a very intense experience, with many kids in a wide range of ages. I don't adjust my talk, but tell them about myself and what I have learned about the winning spirit. They totally identify with it, and at the end they give me a standing ovation. This is an important lesson for me, because I learn that my message isn't relevant only to kids from the inner city, but to all kids. No matter how well off a family may be, being a kid is still a hard job. Almost a full hundred percent of these students will graduate from Poly Prep and attend prestigious colleges. In some ways, it's harder for these kids because so much is expected of them.

About six months later, when the visit has turned into a wonderful memory, Shari calls again. "The kids are still talking about you," she says. "They want to know how they can become part of your next marathon. What can they do to help?"

I agree to come back to see what we can all do together. If my first visit to Poly Prep was intense, my second blows me away. There are posters in the hall saying WELCOME HOME, ZOE! In chapel, a representative of each class comes up and presents me with a handmade card or gift or poster. One is a kind of sandwich board with a big turtle on one side and the signatures of all the kids in the class on the other. They are all one-of-a-kind genuine gifts of the spirit.

The student from each class who makes the presentation is one who has survived some personal trauma or serious challenge by rising to the occasion since the last time I was there. This was not a program that was decided on at lunch the day before. It was well thought out and planned, and a lot of heart went into it.

We decide that a good thing for the students to do should require planning, dedication, ingenuity, and a lot of persistence and hard work. After consulting with Dick Traum at Achilles, I encourage them to participate in the Endow a Chair Program, which raises money to buy wheelchairs for disabled Achilles athletes. The students are in wholehearted agreement and can't wait to get started.

Participating in this program will not be an overnight affair. A top-of-the-line racing chair costs several thousand dollars, and even though Poly Prep goes from grades five through twelve, the student body is not large.

They find they can do a host of things to raise the money. The project in many ways begins to parallel the marathon. There are times when they think maybe they have bitten off more than they can chew. There are times when they wonder if they'll ever make it to the finish line. It becomes the ultimate test not only of their persistence and ingenuity, but of their faith as well.

Kathy Rienzi, the French teacher, becomes the unofficial chairperson of the fund-raising effort. She is determined that this will be a commitment not to be taken lightly, fall by the wayside, or get lost in the shuffle. She is adamant that it will not suffer the fate that befalls so many of our good intentions when the daily grind of reality sets in. Kathy keeps the kids on target and accountable, moving slowly and surely toward their goal.

Dorothy Donovan, chairperson of the Math department, comes up with the idea of Hat Day. Normally there are strict dress codes, which are rigorously enforced. But on that designated day, students will be able to purchase for only one dollar the privilege of wearing the hat of their choice. Hat Day is a phenomenal success, raising more than $400.

Lori Redell, head of admissions, presides over a gala bake sale that involves the wholehearted efforts of all the kids and their parents and the entire teaching staff. And when all the quarters and dimes and dollars have been counted, it brings them more than $500 closer to their goal.

Nicole Buk, chairperson of the Language department, donates a Jackie Onassis auction ticket, whose sale raises another $500.

Vivian Ross, a parent of one of the students, has a contact with the Hygeia Medical Company and is able to get a considerable price break on the wheelchair.

After six months of unrelenting hard work, they raised more than $2500. Enough money to buy not one, but two brand-new racing wheelchairs.

And so I am invited back to Poly Prep and morning chapel for a third time. This time, it is to accept delivery of the wheelchairs on behalf of Achilles and the Endow a Chair Program and to share with the kids and teachers what I know of the recipient of one of the chairs. I tell them what I know of Michael Inglese, who, by anyone's standards, has had a difficult life. His mother died when he was still a boy and his father pretty much abandoned him. At the age of twelve, he suffered a brain tumor, the complications of which left him facially disfigured and permanently in a wheelchair. In addition to this, he lives with the daily challenges of cerebral palsy.

In spite of everything, in 1995 he attempted to run his first marathon. He had to drop out at the twentieth mile, a heartbreaking 6.2 miles short of the finish line. His wheelchair had broken down, and he was defeated by the extreme cold. Now, thanks to the students of Poly Prep, 1996 will be another chapter in his marathon adventures, one with a far different ending.

I tell them I have had the pleasure of speaking to Michael on the phone and found him to be a quiet man of great endurance and simple faith. Much of his time is spent training or working with the other parishioners of the Holy Cross Episcopal Church in his hometown of Kingston, New York. Although he is shy and reticent and, as a rule, not given to public appearances or ceremonies of any kind, in a couple of weeks he makes an exception. He journeys from Kingston to Poly Prep, accompanied by his friend and pastor, the indomitable Father Frank Wellner. And on that day, the students of Poly Prep get to experience firsthand the effect of what they have achieved.

And so on this morning, on this special third visit to the chapel, I try to share, with words I cannot find, what the gift of the wheelchairs has meant to me.

For many years, like most of us, I have watched the news and read the papers with a growing sense of helplessness and hopelessness. I wanted to change the world. I wanted to put on a super cape and go out and fight crime. I wanted to bring a swift and expedient end to the reign of violence and drugs that is slaughtering our children and threatening the fabric of our future. I wanted to be the President and immediately pass the legislation that would feed the hungry, shelter the homeless, and wipe out bigotry and hate; political parties and fiscal budgets be damned. And because I could not do *everything,* I came to believe that I could not do *anything.* And that just isn't true.

All of us are capable of doing *something* every day of our lives. Part of my *something* is the marathon and all the activities it has given birth to. Everyone can find and create that special *something* in their own lives. And perhaps this is the definition of Global Empowerment in its simplest and purest form: the ability to leave the planet a little better at night than we found it in the morning.

So, for me, the gift of the wheelchairs is ultimately an act of Global Empowerment. It is a gift of far more than just two pieces of equipment. It represents both magic and enormous effort. It represents the stories of the kids and their commitment to making this a better planet. It represents the exhilaration it will bring to the recipients, the stories they'll have to share, and the thrill it will bring to the spectators who watch them go by.

At the end of my acceptance speech, I tell them to get on their feet and give themselves and each other a standing ovation; I tell them that the energy of that ovation will reverberate in this chapel forever and ever and will always be a part of the rich history of Poly Prep. They have done something special, and it matters.

Chapter 15

Sometimes friendship is an event and sometimes it's a process. When friendship is a process, there is a great deal of tolerance and negotiation. Political beliefs and philosophical orientations are endlessly discussed and dissected. Differences and similarities are noted and catalogued in the recesses of memory, to be reviewed and re-examined at some future date.

Transcendence is the hallmark of friendship as an event. It's the instantaneous recognition of a kindred spirit. It supersedes the boundaries of race, religion, politics, and sexual orientation. And every once in a while, it even defies the dictates of common sense.

Michael Hurley and I are a friendship event. The minute we met, we were friends. Just like that. None of the usual semantic posturing and unconscious testing that goes on in the initial stages of most relationships. It was pure and simple, a matter of Kismet and Karma.

For us, there was instant recognition. As though we were two five-year-olds finding each other in the playground. No matter what adult significance our friendship would acquire over the years, there was always that essential element of innocence and playfulness.

It is 1989, and Michael is the second-shift supervisor at Tiger Information Systems in New York City. Tiger is a twenty-four-hour-a-day temporary placement agency that supplies top-of-the-line word processors and desktop graphic specialists to law firms, investment banks, and other prestigious clients. It also has a permanent placement division and a training division that services several hundred clients in the metropolitan area.

I am hired as the third-shift supervisor and begin work on February 14. People always kid me about being Cupid's valentine present to Tiger.

When I am hired, I don't tell them I have multiple sclerosis. I know that I can do this job better than anyone can. I'm afraid that if they find out I have MS, they won't give me the chance to prove myself. I'm afraid that somewhere in the back of their minds they may think that it makes me less than I am.

Of all the lethal disorders that afflict the human spirit, I think that prejudice is the worst and most insidious. It is a silent, invisible killer that blinds the soul and paralyzes the spirit. It leaves us unwilling and unable to accept that which is not a mirror image of ourselves. Sometimes it may not be conscious, but it could certainly be the death penalty for my future at Tiger. I'm not willing to take that risk.

I buy a black folding cane. Before I go upstairs each day, I reduce it to smaller proportions and hide it in my knapsack. Although I do walk with a serious limp, I'm familiar enough with human nature to know that no one will ask me about it. It would be considered bad manners. Tacky at best. I hope that my hunch is right and I can buy myself some much-needed time.

My first few weeks at Tiger are spent in training; my time split between the first and second shifts. Each shift has a unique set of functions and responsibilities that contribute to the whole being more than the sum of its parts.

As second-shift supervisor, Michael takes me under his wing and schools me in the fine arts of Tiger Temps. He teaches me about individual clients and their various predilections. He also teaches me a great deal about life as a temp.

Like me, he values having a permanent, full-time job where he can show up day after day. There's something to be said for collecting a paycheck at the end of every week and building long-term relationships with co-workers. He also understands the value of transience. He gives me a whole different philosophy on how to view the temporary employment industry.

He explains that some people get into it because they're "in the arts," and this pays the bills between gigs. And some people get into it for the sheer adventure of showing up at a different place every day.

By my set of values, I don't see it as an adventure at all. Walking into a new set of expectations and personalities every day is not my idea of the good life. It's tantamount to hell on earth. But Michael helps me see the world through their eyes, and I become a better player in their adventure. He teaches me what companies to send them to, and what will work and what won't, based on their personalities and career goals. He helps me redefine the words *challenge* and *diversity*.

I am at Tiger about three months when the inevitable happens. A temp walks into the office and recognizes me from a small TV piece that was done after my first marathon. My worst fear has come true. Now everyone will know I have MS.

Much to my relief and amazement, my co-workers are absolutely thrilled. They can't get enough stories about why I run and how I train and what it's like to be out there all night putting in the miles. There is a healthy curiosity about the ins and outs of MS and none of the negative judgments or presuppositions I had feared.

As time passes and I become more proficient at my job, Michael and I begin to talk a little bit less about work and a little bit more about ourselves and our lives. Sometimes I come in a half-hour early, and sometimes he stays a half-hour late. One way or another, we always make the time.

In the course of our discussions, we realize that we both write. I write well but sporadically, constantly waiting for the muse to show up. Michael is more prolific. He is talented but shy about his work. Sometimes he calls me up in the middle of the night and reads me something he has just written. I title those poems "Hot off the Hurley Press" till he finds more suitable names for them. Of all that he has shared with me, this is one of my all-time favorites.

Homeless
Hair like frayed Velcro patches
clings to his scalp.
Hepatic eyes dart aimlessly.
With a withered donut in one hand
and a haggard newspaper
tucked under his arm
He paces.
The subway car rocks
to his psychotic cadence.
I strain to hear the words
that drip from his mouth.
I see the shell of humanity.
Crisp with filth
the brown polyester sweater

encases his fragile frame.
Shiny with pain
the slickered black blue pants
drip uneasily from his hips.
I sit frozen
unable to move
in his home.

One night as he's on his way out the door, he turns on his heel and says "Oh, by the way, I think that you should know that I'm HIV positive." A parting shot, and then he's gone. I realize he's deliberately staged it this way. No time for reactions or discussion.

We don't speak that night. Given the enormity of what he's just told me, there isn't much to say. I guess he wants to give me time to process this piece of information. I know he'll bring it up again when he's ready to talk about it, and I don't want to push him. I realize his telling me is an act of trust and emotional intimacy. It strengthens the fabric of our friendship. After that night never again do I attempt to disguise my cane. Not for anyone. Not for any reason. I don't have to. I can take the risk now.

In the years that follow, our friendship deepens. We talk a great deal about living and a great deal about dying. We both know that in the face of any potentially serious disease, the possibility of one does not exist without the reality of the other. Sometimes we talk heart to heart, and sometimes we get rowdy and silly, making up nonsensical epitaphs and ridiculous last wills and testaments. And sometimes, for weeks or even months, there is no talk of either HIV or MS.

There are a number of emotional parallels between his

HIV and my multiple sclerosis. Michael has reached the same conclusion in his life that I had earlier reached in mine: you can't spend your whole life either waiting to die or waiting for a cure. If you do that, you have no life at all. You don't just have a disease; you become one.

Over the years, Michael's health declines. In 1992 he has a severe bout of pneumonia. It is followed by chemotherapy for the treatment of Karposi's syndrome. His immune system becomes weaker and weaker. At one point, he has three T cells left. He calls them the Three Stooges.

This is a hard time not only for Michael, but for everyone at Tiger Temps who knows and loves him. Nothing drastic has ever befallen a Tiger employee before. There are no rule books. We are all flying by the seat of our pants, making it up as we go along, and praying to God that we're getting it right. The word *improvisation* takes on brand-new meaning in all our lives.

I have always believed that the people at Tiger, managers and staff alike, behave the way people ought to behave in life. They work hard. They play fair. They treat one another well. They listen if someone has something to say. There is great value placed on loyalty and team work. Not just as an abstract concept based on self-serving rhetoric and convenience, but as a living bond that melds people together through both the good times and the bad.

Tiger keeps Michael on the payroll at his full weekly salary for almost a year after he is unable to work full time. Not only do they "talk the talk," but they back it up with action. Integrity taken to such an extreme is a rare commodity in corporate America. There are hospital visits and endless phone calls. Finally, Michael becomes too ill to continue living in New York on his own. He returns to Texas to live with his family. They are a great source of comfort and support for him.

He calls me frequently from Texas, on my shift and in the middle of the night. In our early conversations we vacillate between two scenarios. He talks about recovering and moving back to New York, and sometimes he talks about dying. At the time they seem to be equal possibilities.

As we approach the final summer of his life, he talks less and less about getting better. He knows that his family and friends want him to keep talking about the future. What they don't understand is that he *is* talking about the future—his future. He's talking about his death.

As much as I hate the thought of letting him go, I realize that the most important gift I can give him is to bear witness to the working-out of his dying process. If it is inevitable, let it be as unique and as amazing as his life has been. Sometimes the best we can do in life is to give those we love as much support in their leaving as we do in their staying.

One night toward the end of the summer, Michael calls me in the middle of the night. He is sitting in the back yard gazing at the summer sky, saying it is one of the things he'll miss the most when he dies.

I realize that, with these words, he has opened a door for me. With faltering steps and heavy heart, I enter, unsure of where the path will lead me. Tentatively I tell him, "Michael, I'll miss you. Where do you think you'll go when you die? If only I could know where you were, I'd feel better about your going."

There is a long silence. Finally he says in a voice of total wonder, "I'm sitting here looking up at all these stars. And that's where I'm going to go. I just know it. I'm going to be up there in the solar system with all those stars. I'll miss the sky, but in exchange for it, I'll be given the galaxy. And you've gotta admit, that's a hell of a trade-in deal." Both of us are crying. Never again do we speak of his getting better or of his returning to New York.

Michael gets all his paper work in order. He makes sure that he will not be subjected to inordinate amounts of useless treatments and that—most important of all—he will not be resuscitated. We talk about ways that he can maintain his dignity and his sense of choice right up to the end. He starts assembling pictures of friends and family to be buried with him. Tactile mementoes of people, places, and moments that have made his life special and precious. Souvenirs of the sacred and the silly. Each bears a memory and a story and all are worth taking on his unknown journey. This is his way of making choices in the face of choicelessness.

I am in touch with him right before the 1992 marathon. He's getting too weary to go on. We both know it. He promises me he'll hold on till I finish the marathon; I tell him that he doesn't have to. He says that he really wants to know that I've completed my marathon before he begins his. We leave it at that.

I have every intention of calling him from the road during the race. In Long Island City, just a bit past the halfway mark, I frantically search for his phone number. In the excitement of the day, I have either lost it or left it home. Directory assistance is of no help. Texas is a big state. A very big state. Since almost all of our contact has been via telephone, for the life of me, I can't remember what town he's in.

All day and all night long, I keep thinking about what that call from the road might mean to him. It isn't that I can tell him anything he doesn't already know. He knows that I love and value him as a friend, but I want to remind him of this in the middle of Marathon Sunday. I want him to be part of this special journey just the way he's let me into his life and given me the privilege of being part of his final journey. He's shared his dreams, his fears, and his feelings with me. I want to return his gift in kind on this, my day of days. And now I can't do that. I don't have the damned phone number, and there's nothing I can do to get it. I can't believe I've been so stupid. I just can't believe it.

After more than twenty-seven hours on the road, I finish the New York City Marathon at around ten on Monday morning. Michael Hurley dies at four o'clock that afternoon.

His mother calls Tiger to let them know. They in turn call me. His mother said he had gone to the bathroom and she was helping him back to bed. He had looked up at her and said, "Mom, I'm just so tired. I really want it to be all over. It's time for me to go." He died in her arms on the floor between the bathroom and the bedroom.

His death is not a surprise, but I am still devastated by it. I can't forgive myself for not bringing his phone number with me to the marathon. I know I'm holding it way out of context, but I just can't get past it. How could I have been so stupid?

My apartment is right over a bar. That very night they begin playing Michael's favorite song on the jukebox. "Crazy," by Patsy Cline. They play it over and over till I think I will either go crazy or run screaming from my apartment.

The song becomes an audio accusation. It's a melodic recrimination for the forgotten phone number, for having

let Michael down. I discount all the other acts of friendship
and love that I showed him in his lifetime. I boil it down
to this one failure. My failure to call him from the course
that day. I wear it like the proverbial albatross. That failure
becomes a bitter taste in the back of my throat that will not
go away.

I find out when Michael's memorial service is to be held
in Texas, and at exactly the same time I hold my personal
service for him here in New York. Remembering all too
vividly our late summer conversation about the stars, I buy
a white candle and a box of those gummy stars that teachers
give the kids on test papers in school. I cover the candle
with those stars. Then I light it and watch it burn down as
I pray for Michael. I sit with it and my memories for a time
and then let it burn itself out as I go on with my household
chores.

When I return, I find that the candle has melted down,
but the stars remain intact. Perfect little psychedelic con-
stellations shining brilliantly in a puddle of white wax.

EVERY YEAR BETWEEN the end of November and the
middle of December I make what I've come to think of as
my Christmas pilgrimage. Across the street from my house
is Stuyvesant Town, a middle-income housing development. That's where I go each year to gaze at the Christmas
lights. This year is no different.

This yearly pilgrimage serves as an opportunity to remi-
nisce about the year that is ending and to dream and plan
for the year ahead. It is a leisurely journey that fully engages
my spirit as well as my body.

First things first. I start with the ground-floor lights.
They are like the easy charm of handsome men or beautiful

women when they enter a room. They momentarily dazzle and beguile, leaving me riveted and breathless.

After a moment or two, my senses readjust, my gaze wanders, and my yearly search begins. Onward and upward. Fifth floor. Eighth floor. Tenth floor. And all that lies between.

Oh, the spectacle of all those lights. The purity of the whites. The glory of the blues. The passion of the reds. The cookie-cutter designs of snowmen and Christmas trees. The free-style zigzags and curlicues. The luminous hieroglyphic signatures of those who dwell behind the window panes.

Even behind drawn curtains and closed venetian blinds, lights continue to blaze. I have always believed that those top-floor alchemists weave their supernatural spells not only with their own pleasure and gratification in mind, but with an intimate knowledge of the inner workings of magic.

Those lights become a beacon for those of us whom life has taught, by either luck or necessity, to dig a little deeper and to look a little higher. They are the jackpot win for those street-level pilgrims like myself who have learned to seek their pleasures not solely from the easy access offerings of life. They are an anthem for those of us whose reach will perpetually exceed our grasp. They are part of the ineffable fabric of magic that binds us to the planet and to each other as surely and simply as muscle and tendon adhere to bone.

The pragmatist in me argues against the inordinate investment of meaning in the everyday stuff and nonsense of life. But the poet and dreamer live on.

In the midst of all this, there is still the overwhelming grief and sense of loss. There is still the memory of Michael.

And then it dawns on me that Michael, in a way, has become just like those tenth-floor Christmas tree lights. No more easy ground-floor access. No more phone calls. No more poetry readings in the middle of the night. But the memory of who he was and the gifts he gave me will always be here. All I'll ever have to do to find them is to look a little higher and to dig a little deeper.

Michael taught me that the moments we cherish and the people we love are never really lost; they transform themselves into another shape or form that we may not immediately recognize. As long as I have the memory of him, and pass on to others the gifts he gave to me, some part of him will live forever.

Michael taught me the values and the virtues of paradox. He was a study of choice in the face of choicelessness. And even in the process of dying, he was more alive than anyone I had ever known.

I believe there is that deeper part of ourselves that reaches out into the world and pulls people in to befriend us, to love us, and to teach us. Michael and I have had parallel lives in ways that we never could have predicted or foreseen when we first met. We were bound together as friends by our internal five-year-olds, our shared sense of poetry and metaphor and our firsthand knowledge of mortality.

After the night of the Christmas lights, I never again hear the Patsy Cline song in the bar downstairs. Maybe the person who played it so often doesn't work or drink there anymore. Coincidence. Maybe. And then again, maybe not.

Four months after his death, there is a memorial service for Michael at the Cathedral of St. John the Divine, in New

York City. Great thought and care go into its planning and execution. All his favorite co-workers from Tiger are there. All the favorite temps whom he serviced so well and cared for so much. His favorite music from classical to country. The Patsy Cline song is played. I am finally able to smile. There is an enormous array of food and beverages. Memories are shared. There is a great deal of laughter. And still there are tears.

Toward the end of the service, I read a poem I have written. The one that Michael liked best. For all time let it stand as a tribute to a special friend and mentor whom I will remember all the days of my life with a tear and a smile.

You are the pain, O Lord,
and You, Great God, are the promise.
You are the memory of love and perfection lost.
You are the dream, long remembered yet half
   forgotten,
whose ashes smolder in my soul,
endlessly igniting, dying, and rekindling.
You are the healing power, an energy pure and
   simple,
infusing my life with Your love and Your laughter,
like the first breath of springtime breathing joy
into the ice-crusted lungs of winter.
You are the Lord my God.
The Master of my life and the keeper of my dreams.
And everything I could ever hope to be, O Lord,
belongs to and is of You.

CHAPTER 16

THE PICTURE IS beautiful, the most honest and real picture anyone has ever taken of me. In every stark detail, it pulses with the vision of Annie Liebovitz, the great portrait photographer. She had spent the better part of an afternoon shooting the endless rolls of film that would produce this picture. The shoot was so much fun. I felt alive. I felt sexy. I felt determined. I felt triumphant.

And now I have this wonderful picture in my hands, and I am devastated. I cry myself to sleep that night.

In two days, on the Friday before the 1996 New York City Marathon, this picture will run in *USA Today* as a full-page ad for the Milk Council. And when it does, the entire country will know exactly who I am. Not my name or what I do, although that information will be there in the copy, in small print. But my most private and personal essence: the real Zoe. It is an image not easy to deal with.

This is not what I had envisioned just a few weeks earlier when my posing for a Milk Ad was first suggested. Until then, something like thirty ads had been done, each featuring a celebrity. Sophia Loren, Cindy Crawford, Spike Lee. The unifying feature was that each person had a milk mustache on his or her upper lip.

The agency that created the campaign is Bozell World Wide. What got them to consider featuring someone who wasn't a celebrity in the ordinary sense of the word was the group called Marathon Strides. Marathon Strides was formed to use the marathon as a fund-raising event for the New York City Chapter of the National MS Society. The group comprises about thirty marathon runners, five of whom have MS. I was the team captain. One of the people on the team had a connection to Bozell World Wide and suggested doing a milk ad showing someone who wasn't a celebrity in the conventional, glitzy sense of the word. Why not publish an ad on the eve of the marathon with someone who has forged her own brand of celebrity by going out and enduring, year after year after year, going on nine years now?

And so I was proposed as the subject, and everyone involved agreed it was a great idea. The $10,000 fee for posing would be donated through Marathon Strides to the New York City Chapter of the MS Society. I was amazed that I'd been asked; I knew what a tremendous honor it was. It would make me not only the first disabled athlete to represent the entire disabled subculture, but also the first regular person to be featured in one of the ads.

I was deeply honored—but also terrified. Unless you're Christie Brinkley, I think anyone's reaction to such a proposal would be "I don't look good enough." Or, "Oh, my God, I'm too old . . . too fat . . . too skinny . . . too ugly . . ." and so on down the list.

Before I could even do the shoot, Annie's production staff asked me to send over some personal letters, photographs, and any other memorabilia that would give her an idea of who I am. They said that Annie does not shoot unless she has a sense of who her subjects are, what matters to them and what they hold precious and real in their life. I decided to send her some of the letters school kids have written to me, along with my journal entries about the marathon. The pictures I sent showed me wearing my shawl and earrings and pins and gewgaws. The whole nine yards. I felt confident that she would get a decent sense of who I am and why the marathon mattered to me. And she would understand that the clothing I intended to show up in is the clothing I actually wear on the road.

Before the shoot, I sent my running clothes out to be cleaned and pressed. I assembled my earrings and pins. The night before, I stayed up, pressing scarves and packing everything in a garment bag. I knew I would change at the studio, so I threw on a wrinkled denim shirt for the ride over there, but I did put on my normal make-up at home; I wanted Annie to see what I looked like in real life.

And now I walk in to the studio, and Annie looks at me with the eyes of the premier photographer she is. I am barely past the door when she announces, "Perfect! That's what you're wearing for the shoot."

I can feel the beginnings of a major headache creeping up the back of my neck. "Annie," I say, trying to press down the sense of panic rising in my voice, "I wouldn't walk my dog in this shirt. I wouldn't be caught dead in this shirt, never mind appearing in a national advertising campaign. I just dragged it out of the dryer and threw it on because everything else I own is in this garment bag. No way!"

Until now, I've been nervous, but the image I have in my mind involves glamour. Lots of glamour. It involves me in my suit jacket and pins and turtle cape. It is the ultimate me, a New York, East Village kind of woman, with maybe a wind machine to blow my hair and scarves around a bit.

New Yorkers will appreciate and probably even recognize my outfit, I reason. It's the real me, and it's exactly how I dress to run.

But Annie's initial reaction to my old shirt sends a jolt of apprehension through me that brings out beads of cold sweat. And again, it's about that criteria of what I'm supposed to look like. It is pointed out to me, and rightly so, that the world is not New York. And while New Yorkers may appreciate my fashion statement, people in other parts of the country may think the wild costume makes me less of an athlete because it doesn't fit *their* picture of how an athlete dresses.

All this is going through my brain at a million miles an hour, and it's giving me palpitations. I'm thinking, "God, if I'm not going to be me, then who am I going to be?" I'll be someone else. I'll end up looking like someone else's version of an athlete. My whole sense of color and style and "Zoe-ness" will be totally lost. I'll be someone else's version of me.

Annie meets my objections by saying that we'll take pictures in my running outfit later. She just wants to shoot a few rolls of me in some plainer clothes as a warm-up—a sort of preliminary shoot to check the lighting and technical details. Then we'll see.

She has bought some clothing herself and asks me to put on a black sweat jacket, with the hood pushed back. I am wearing black tights, and she stands me in front of a background of seamless white paper. No pins. No earrings. No Flash. Just me, Zoe, dressed in black, with the worn-out old sneakers I train in on rainy days. My only other props are my two battered and war-scarred crutches and the ancient pair of fingerless biker's gloves that I've worn through every race. They cushion my hands on the crutch handles and keep my palms from blistering.

Eventually, I change into my own outfit, and the shoot becomes a lot of fun. There's the whole business of the milk mustache, which is actually a concoction of natural dairy products made up by a delightful man everyone calls Mad Norman the Milkman. Mad Norman comes in from California solely to attend to the mustache, and concocts three witches' brew variations of his magic milk formula. Norman is a really wonderful guy, and his nickname is well deserved in the fondest and best way.

That feeling of glamour I had imagined at last becomes real. I am made up, dressed up, and milked up. I am fussed over, fawned over, and given the full star treatment throughout the shoot. Annie is terrific beyond words. She is the consummate artist, demanding and brusque with her staff, yet compassionate and understanding. I feel we form a real bond during the shoot, which turns into a grand and memorable adventure.

I go home, she processes her film, picks some shots, and sends them to Bozell. Two days before the ad is to run, they send me a copy. Expecting to see myself in all my glory, the consummate picture of color, glamour, and glitz, I find—just me! The jewelry is gone; the earrings are gone. All the colors and accessories I have come to value as part of my marathon outfit—all of it gone. There is just me, full-length, dressed in a black-hooded sweat jacket, staring straight ahead. I break down, sobbing.

It is truly a phenomenal picture, one that perhaps only Annie Liebovitz could have made. If I view it objectively, I look strong, I look alive, I look determined. In the tights, you can see the development and definition of my legs. There is no doubt that I have trained hard to be this strong; no one wakes up with legs that muscular. You look at the picture and see my training, every bit of it. The picture is a stunning illumination of my personal achievement.

So why am I having this unreasonably intense reaction to it? I mean, this is not a single tear trickling down my cheek. The flood gates are open and the river has over-flowed its banks. My pillow will soon be declared a national disaster area, eligible for federal aid. I cry for hours over this image. I am beyond reason. I am beyond caring. I am inconsolable.

I cry until it finally dawns on me that it's not just the clothes and the sparkly things that have been taken away. My God, she's even taken away my smile. What she has re-created is the image I see in the morning when I face the mirror. It's me, without the accoutrements, without the packaging. Take all of that away, and it's just me and my crutches.

This is what you get when you strip away all the other stuff. And the crutches look stark, old, and worn against the white background. I know them both so well, and have lived with them for so many years, that I have even named them: Spot and Rover. The arm piece on the left one is bent from the fall I took in 1995. One of the shafts is bent, too. People always tell me to get new ones, but I can't do that. The bends and dents are constant reminders for me to watch out for potholes, both on the road and in life. The gloves are almost as battered as the crutches. There is noth-ing in the picture, not even my smile, to draw the viewer's attention away from who and what I am.

I could not feel more vulnerable if she had photographed

me naked. When I am stripped down that far, there is no smile. No mask. There is just the stark determination I must sometimes summon up not just to do a marathon, but simply to get through the day.

That is exactly what I have always admired about Annie's photographs—her ability to strip away pretense and façade and defenses and get to the real person underneath. Though I knew that going in, I still thought I would be this vision of scarves blowing, shawl billowing, and earrings sparkling. I thought I would see my fantasy picture of myself. The same way I once thought that running the marathon meant getting rid of my crutches and dashing across the finish line like Grete Waitz. I wanted to be beautiful. I wanted to be glamorous. I wanted to be me, only better. Much better.

Even in my shock, I know this is a magnificent picture. There is a great deal of beauty in this picture. And once I am able to deal with my initial reaction, I can take great pride in it and say, "Wow! That's me. That's *really* me!"

But it's a very private me. A private moment captured through my guard. That is the heart of the matter, accepting that everyone who sees the picture will actually know who I am. I mean *really* know who I am. A very private look has now found its way into a very public forum. My being suddenly confronted with that has raised feelings I thought I no longer had. Feelings I thought I had dealt with many, many years ago.

The milk ad picture brought me face to face with the disease and how difficult it has been to live with. What the picture is about is how tired I am of having MS. I'm tired of needing determination to accomplish the most basic tasks of life, those most people take for granted. I'm tired of having to play harder than other people. I'm tired of things taking longer and costing more. Ultimately, some days, I'm tired of just being tired. Sometimes I don't remember when I didn't have MS, because I've had it now for more than half my life. And the look on my face in that picture is a reminder of how much naked determination it takes me to get through life, how much it takes sometimes just to get through the day.

These are the things I don't let most people see. Even during the marathon, when someone comes by with a camera, I dredge up a smile and a one-liner. There's no need to inflict this stuff on the rest of the world. Since their knowing would serve no function whatsoever, why should I flaunt that aspect of me or my life? What good would it do to give them this knowledge anyway? They can't do anything to fix it or change it. It's the kind of thing that makes good people feel bad and may give some others, who wouldn't mind seeing me strike out, a truckload of ammunition.

With my friends, it's a whole other story. The people who do substantial pieces of the marathon with me see that look, because it's real. It's there. My co-workers see it on occasion, too. But in these cases, it becomes part of our shared history. They are no more or less familiar with my "look" than I am with theirs. A certain intimacy forms over the years and the miles, and born of this intimacy are the gifts of comfort and acceptance.

In recent years, during the late stages of the marathon, when I begin to lose my fine coordination and muscle control, I allow my road companions to feed and dress me. Initially, I was resistant, but I've come to learn it's just another thing you do to reach your goal.

Necessity has taught me to lighten up, to let go a little,

and to let others into my equation. It has forced me to take what I see as the greatest personal risk of all. I have dared to become vulnerable, and in the process have learned perhaps some of the greatest lessons of my life. Vulnerability has taught me humility. And humility has blessed me with strength.

At work there is something of a contest every morning when my relief shift comes in to see who gets to help me put my coat on. Some days I can do it myself, but after a full shift, my left arm frequently doesn't like bending back to go through the sleeve, and it's just a whole lot easier if someone grabs the arm and does it for me. But there is an intimacy there as well, a true intimacy, not the "instant" variety we are so fond of in our society.

Then there are the doors to the accounting department. They are made of solid wood and, by my standards, are incredibly heavy. Getting in is relatively easy; I simply lean into the door and throw my entire body weight against it and force it open. Getting out is another story. I have to get it open a crack, wedge my foot into that crack, then work my elbow in, and finally lever myself against the door to force it open.

Every so often, there is the day when, no matter what I do, I can't get the door open. So I ask someone from accounting to let me out. No one minds. They like helping, and it's even become a joke. It's Zoe-and-the-door thing, as compared with Zoe-and-the-coat thing. And I don't mind their helping me. Not at all.

Sometimes that door is just a door, a minor nuisance of no real consequence, just another daily exercise in improvisation and ingenuity. When I can't open it, I ask someone who can, and that's that. No big deal. And sometimes that door takes on a life of its own. It becomes a metaphor for all the doors in my life, on every level, that are just too damned heavy and too damned difficult to open—and yet I must keep going through them.

In that way, the marathon is much easier than real life, precisely because it isn't real. It costs me a lot to get to the starting line and a lot to finish, but it's something I choose to do. The day-to-day stuff is just there, all the time, unrelenting and merciless. No matter what else I may choose to do in life, I've still got to deal with it.

Ultimately, that's what the milk picture turned out to be. It confronted me with my I-can't-open-the-door look, and it brought all the frustration of all the years flooding over me. In the long run, it was a once-in-a-lifetime opportunity to learn a little, to grow a little, and to heal a lot.

Other people saw different issues. Many thought I should have felt that I was being exploited as a member of the disabled subculture. Some interviewers asked me if I felt deliberately manipulated. The answer is no, not at all. I feel honored, not used. To be the first is special, and if there needs to be a trail blazer, let it be me. I hope that someday seeing disabled people in ads becomes so normal, you won't even notice. But like everything else in life, it's got to start somewhere.

I should have known that when the ad did run, others would not share my reaction at all. As with so many other things, they made up their own reality. Almost everyone loved it. Some of my friends, instead of seeing the vulnerability I felt, saw total "New York attitude." My co-workers hung it on the wall of the office, where it remains. Some have even sworn that my eyes follow them around the room. Strangers in elevators, laundromats, and grocery stores have asked if I am the woman in the ad. And during the marathon, a remarkable number of people rooted me on by yelling, "Go, Milk, Go!"

The disabled community as a whole took a great deal of well-deserved pride in the ad. It was about as mainstream and in-your-face as any of us can get. There were the inevitable few who wanted to know, "Why her? Why not me?" And the bottom line on that was, who can say? To tell you the truth, I don't really know.

The world is full of people who think they should have the TV show, the book, or the movie about their lives. Who knows? Maybe they should. The funny thing is that I never thought I should have any of those things. Getting them was never my goal. And maybe that's why I was asked to do the milk ad. Maybe that's why I'm talking about it right now.

But the ad and the book, and whatever may come from them down the road, change nothing. With or without them, I will still be doing what I do—running the marathon, spending time with kids in schools, and basking in the life all around me.

I can honestly say that, even with all my ups and downs, I wouldn't swap lives with anyone. Not even for a minute. Over the years and the miles, I've had a lot of splendid adventures with a lot of wonderful people. And in my way, I've tried to make things a little better, whenever and wherever I could. And every once in a while I've gotten lucky. Really lucky.

And if my life suddenly ended tomorrow, it would end with few regrets. I could never say that I haven't had my fair portion of all the good stuff. Because I really have. And while I may not have had my fill, God knows I've had my share.

CHAPTER 17

I HAVE ALWAYS believed that each of us has a personal theme song. It speaks of who we are and where we've been, and, perhaps more important, of who we may yet become and where the road may lead us.

For many years my personal theme song was "Tomorrow," from the Broadway play *Annie*. I have always believed that if we can hold on for just one more day, there is always the possibility of change—the promise of reversal and the joy of renewal. Such is the potential magic inherent in the promise of "Tomorrow."

And then, several years ago, when my marathon adventures began, I found a second theme song. It was "One Moment in Time," the mega-hit originally recorded by Whitney Houston. From the first time I heard it, it seemed as though the chorus had been written just for me.

> Give me one moment in time
> When I'm more than I thought I could be
> When all of my dreams are a heartbeat away
> And the answers are all up to me.
> Give me one moment in time
> When I'm racing with destiny
> And in that one moment of time
> I will be—I will be free.

In every race that I run and every line that I cross there is for me that Moment in Time—that winning moment of power and pleasure and grace. It's not a snapshot moment to be filed in the recesses of memory. It's a Technicolor moment of self-excedence and self-acceptance. It's a living moment of resource and possibility. It's a veritable encyclopedia of self-knowledge, a reference point from which to create and re-create that winning moment in all areas of my life.

And so, each year, I continue to cross the finish line. With head thrown back and right arm raised in victory, I shout, "Yes" to the morning sky. It is one of the smallest words in the English language but also one of the largest. It is a word of infinite power and possibility.

There is a poster scotch-taped to my bedroom wall. It is the last thing I see before falling asleep and the first thing I see on rising. It is a picture of a nameless, faceless runner on what appears to be an endless road.

The sentiment inscribed on the poster is as follows:

The race belongs not only to
the swift and strong—
but to those who keep on running.

Words to Live By . . .